The Kingdom Within

David Chapman, D.Min.

The Kingdom Within

David Chapman

TRU Publishing
1726 S. 1st Ave.
Safford, Arizona 85546

Table of Contents

Introduction

The terms "Kingdom of God" and "Kingdom of Heaven" are interchangeable in the Gospels. The latter is used only by Matthew in his Gospel (32 times) because the term was more amenable to the Jewish audience to whom he was writing. The phrase Kingdom of God is used 67 times in the New Testament. Together, the phrase is used 99 times.

Jesus began His public ministry by proclaiming that the Kingdom of God was at hand.

> **Matthew 4:17 From that time Jesus began to preach and to say, "Repent, for the kingdom of heaven is at hand."**

The verb "at hand" (*eggizo*) means "extreme closeness, immediate imminence." Yet, Jesus was not speaking of a physical, earthly Kingdom. The Jews were looking for a Messiah who would deliver them from the oppression of Rome and setup a physical Kingdom. But Jesus came the first time with a different mission – to suffer and die for the sins of the world and rise again. The Kingdom was in their presence, but they missed it. Many today place their emphasis on looking for the outward Kingdom. They constantly interpret the news of the day and set dates for His coming. Jesus said, "Therefore you also be ready, for the Son of Man is coming at an hour you do not expect" (Luke 12:40).

The Amplified translation provides an elaboration on the verb *repent*:

> **Matthew 4:17 (AMP) From that time Jesus began to preach and say, "Repent [change your inner self—your old way of thinking, regret past sins, live your life in a way that proves repentance; seek God's purpose for your life], for the kingdom of heaven is at hand."**

Because of the proximity of the Kingdom of God, our lives should not remain in the same sinful condition. Repentance is a natural response to the presence of God.

The following preachers of the Gospel of the Kingdom all began their ministries with the same single word – "Repent!"

- John the Baptist (Matthew 3:1-2)
- Jesus (Matthew 4:17)
- The Twelve (Mark 6:12)
- The Disciples after the Resurrection (Luke 24:46-47)
- The first sermon of the Church (Peter) on the Day of Pentecost (Acts 2:38)
- The Apostle Paul (Acts 26:19-20)

Repentance is an attitude that should be continuous – always turning away and denying self and turning to God. John the Baptist understood the power of the Kingdom. When he saw the King, he declared, "He must increase, but I must decrease."

The focus of this book on the Kingdom of God will be the inward and invisible aspects of the Kingdom. Topics such as the following, as well as many others, will be covered:

- The difference between Kingdom living and religion
- Finding your personal assignment in the Kingdom
- The signs and miracles of the Kingdom
- The enemies of the Kingdom
- The authority of the Kingdom
- God's provision in the Kingdom
- The coming physical Kingdom
- How to advance the Kingdom of God

The New Testament Greek word for "kingdom" is *basileia* and means, "The realm over which a sovereign exercises his authority." We will be seeking to understand the spiritual dynamics of that realm and the practical applications of living in that realm.

The subject of the Kingdom of God is so important that we find Jesus, after His resurrection, giving the disciples a 40-day education on the Kingdom of God.

Acts 1:1-3
1 The former account I made, O Theophilus, of all that Jesus began both to do and teach, 2 until the day in which He was taken up, after He through the Holy Spirit had given commandments to the apostles whom He had chosen, 3 to whom He also presented Himself alive after His suffering by many infallible proofs, being seen by them during forty days and speaking of the things pertaining to the kingdom of God.

The Gospels contain the record of the earthly ministry and mission of Jesus. It was the beginning of the education of the disciples – like an under-graduate degree, if you will. This 40-day, intense, in-depth training on the Kingdom of God was like a graduate level program for these men, prior to the release of their ministries to change the world.

The Kingdom of God is Within You

> **Luke 17:20-21**
> **20 Now when He was asked by the Pharisees when the kingdom of God would come, He answered them and said, "The kingdom of God does not come with observation; 21 nor will they say, 'See here!' or 'See there!' For indeed, the kingdom of God is within you."**

This is not the answer that the Pharisees were looking for. In fact, most of the questions that were asked by the Pharisees were setup questions to trip Jesus up in some way. Their hearts were not set to seek God. They asked the question of *when* the Kingdom would come, when the Kingdom was in their very presence. The Kingdom of God is hidden from the *what, when, where* seekers and only revealed to the *Who* seekers.

Pharisees cannot enter the Kingdom for their focus is outward. Jesus said, "Now you Pharisees make the outside of the cup and dish clean, but your inward part is full of greed and wickedness" (Luke 11:39).

Pharisees were the elite religious group of Jesus' day. They actually ushered in a religious revolution between 200-300 B.C. They were very devout in their beliefs and practices. Pharisees would pray up to nine hours a day and fast twice a week. They often memorized the entire first five books of the Law (Genesis, Exodus, Leviticus, Numbers and Deuteronomy).

However, Pharisees also made up a lot of *extra* rules to go along with the Word of God. For instance, they had approximately two thousand rules just related to the Sabbath. It's a never-ending dilemma when one seeks to define what constitutes *work*. This is an area that the Pharisees were always trying to trip Jesus up so that they would have grounds for accusation.

Even today, Orthodox Jews adhere to very strict Sabbath rules. For instance, if a Doctor, who is an Orthodox Jew, writes a prescription on the Sabbath, he must do so with his left hand (if right-handed). If he makes a house call, he must leave the car running while inside. Religious people have had 3,500 years to add man-made rules to the Law and burden God's people down. Sadly, this same gospel of works has crept into the Church and deceived people into thinking that salvation is earned through good works.

The Pharisees made serving God an obligation. Jesus told them in Luke 11:46, "For you crush people with unbearable religious demands, and you never lift a finger to ease the burden" (NLT). God doesn't want His people coming to church, reading the Bible, praying and sharing the Gospel out of obligation.

The Pharisees were entirely focused on the outward. They loved to be seen of men, get the best seats, and be served. They had these things called *phylacteries* that were small, square, leather boxes with portions of the Law written inside. They strapped them to their foreheads and their left arms.

In His fiery sermon in Matthew 23, Jesus called Pharisees the following names:

- Hypocrites (v 13)
- Sons of hell (v 15)
- Blind guides (v 16)
- Fools (v 17)
- Whitewashed tombs (v 27)
- Serpents (v 33)
- Vipers (v 33)
- Murderers (v 35)

We must guard our hearts to prevent a religious spirit like the Pharisees from developing in our hearts and attitudes. You may say that the adjectives that Jesus used in Matthew 23 don't describe you, but understand that this religious spirit is very subtle. Remember, the Pharisees were highly esteemed as the religious leaders of Jesus' day.

How to tell if you are developing a religious spirit like the Pharisees:

- Focusing too much on minor differences in doctrine and practice
- Becoming more judgmental toward others
- Mistaking personal preferences for the Holy Spirit

- Allowing the external to be more important than the internal
- Creating new rules for every situation
- Seeking to control people
- Serving God becomes burdensome for self and others you influence
- Always seeking man's approval rather than God's

If these or other similar characteristics are starting to manifest in your life, ask God to deliver you from the inner Pharisee! Our goal should be to follow the believers' creed from the 1600's, the time period of the Protestant Reformation:

In Essentials Unity
In Non-Essentials Liberty
In All Things Charity [Love]

If we can get the Kingdom of God inside of people, through the New Birth, transformation will commence from the inside out. In Matthew chapter 13, Jesus tells several parables about the Kingdom; one of them was about the mustard seed. Jesus said that the Kingdom of Heaven is like a mustard seed. He said that though it was the least of all the seeds, when it is grown it is greater than the herbs and becomes a tree (v 31-32). Change and growth happen over time as a new believer applies the proper nurturing. Eventually, the Kingdom of God will infiltrate every area of the person's life.

See Here

> Nor will they say, 'See here!' or 'See there!' For indeed, the kingdom of God is within you."

'See here!' or 'See there!' While we can draw upon examples, the Kingdom is not a man, a movement or a denomination. Too often, we place our eyes upon someone because they are used by God or are greatly anointed. I know people who will travel hundreds of miles to be prayed for by a famous healing evangelist, but will not exercise faith in God's Word in their everyday life.

Further, we cannot afford to take on the attitude that only *our group* can be used by God. The disciples once asked a man to stop casting out devils in Jesus' name because he was not one of the Twelve.

> Mark 9:38 (NLT) "Teacher, we saw someone using your name to cast out demons, but we told him to stop because he wasn't in our group."

Jesus, seeing the small-mindedness of the disciples told them, "Don't stop him! Anyone who is not against us is for us" (v 39-40). We cannot allow ourselves to get caught up in the pride of believing that God is using only us.

The mission of the local church is to be both *radiant* and *relevant*. That is, radiant with God's glory and presence and relevant with the Gospel – pertinent to people's daily lives. The two should not be exclusive of one another. The old phrase of being "too heavenly minded for any earthly good" does not apply to true Kingdom living. The closer we get to God, the more profound of an impact we can have on people.

> **Acts 4:13 Now when they saw the boldness of Peter and John, and perceived that they were uneducated and untrained men, they marveled. And they realized that they had been with Jesus.**

The Invisible Kingdom

The Invisible Kingdom: "Invisible" means "obscure, concealed, unseen." The world around us cannot see the Kingdom and its principles are foreign. Jesus said that it *does not come with observation*.

Man has tried to prove or disprove God with the intellect for thousands of years. The problem is that to the natural mind – the intellect, God and His ways – the principles of His Kingdom, are foolishness.

> **1 Corinthians 2:14 (MSG) The unspiritual self, just as it is by nature, can't receive the gifts of God's Spirit. There's no capacity for them.**

The New Testament believer must learn to walk by a higher order – by the Holy Spirit. *For as many as are led by the Spirit of God, they are the sons of God* (Romans 8:14). The Greek word for "sons" means "position of privilege." Kingdom living is about progressively entering greater levels of privilege. This comes about through obedience and faithfulness.

Privilege means appropriating and enjoying all of the blessings that God has provided for his children. Just because a person is a believer – a Christian, does not by default mean that he or she will lead a victorious life. In fact, Paul wrote that an heir, if he remains in ignorance of his inheritance, would live a life that does not differ from a slave, even though, legally, he is the possessor of all (Galatians 4:1).

Rickey Henderson, the Hall of Fame baseball player, once received a bonus check from the Oakland A's for one million dollars. This was during the early 1980's, when players weren't making millions of dollars. Mr. Henderson, instead of depositing the large check, framed it and hung it on his wall. He was so proud of finally being a millionaire that he wanted all to see it. After some time went by, the finance people for the A's alerted ownership that the check had not cleared. They in turn called Rickey and requested that he cash the check! The moral to the story is that unless you deposit, or apply, what has been granted you, there is no effect on your lifestyle.

The reason that unbelievers cannot see the Kingdom of God is because Satan has blinded their minds to the truth.

> **2 Corinthians 4:4 Whose minds the god of this age has blinded, who do not believe, lest the**

light of the gospel of the glory of Christ, who is the image of God, should shine on them.

Believers, on the other hand, have the ability to spiritually see what cannot be seen with the human eye.

> **2 Corinthians 4:18 While we do not look at the things which are seen, but at the things which are not seen. For the things which are seen are temporary, but the things which are not seen are eternal.**

The "see it to believe it" approach is denied the privileges, advantages and opportunities of the Kingdom. The enlightened believer walks with the Title Deed of everything that has been divinely guaranteed within the Kingdom.

> **Hebrews 11:1 (Amplified) Now faith is the assurance (title deed, confirmation) of things hoped for (divinely guaranteed), and the evidence of things not seen [the conviction of their reality—faith comprehends as fact what cannot be experienced by the physical senses].**

Kingdom living is not done so through the five senses. These are what the body needs to function in the natural world. But the spiritual world – the sphere or realm over which a sovereign exercises His authority – requires faith.

Not of this World

> **"My kingdom is not of this world" Jesus, John 18:36.**

The following can be stated regarding Jesus' declaration that His Kingdom was not of this world:

- It is not worldly or political by *nature.*
- It is not of a worldly or human *origin.*
- It cannot be *defined, measured or quantified* by worldly standards.
- There are no *limitations or boundaries* of where the Kingdom of God can have impact.

As Kingdom people, we must maintain the mindset of a sojourner here on this earth. We are just passing through. It is not our mission to build a kingdom unto ourselves, but instead to advance the Kingdom of God in the hearts of people.

This is what Jesus said about His followers (different translations added for comparison):

John 17:16
- *They are not of the world, just as I am not of the world (NLT).*
- *They are no more defined by the world than I am defined by the world (Message)*
- *They don't belong to this world, and neither do I (CEV).*

Become "God-inside-minded"

Christians should be *God-inside-minded*, in that the Holy Spirit lives in each believer.

> **1 Corinthians 6:19 Or do you not know that your body is the temple of the Holy Spirit who is in you, whom you have from God, and you are not your own?**

> **1 Corinthians 3:16 Do you not know that you are the temple of God and that the Spirit of God dwells in you?**

Our lives are empowered by the Holy Spirit. If a person gets born again – born from above, as Jesus described in John 3, the Holy Spirit takes up residence in the body of the believer. Further, there is a subsequent work of the Holy Spirit known as the Baptism with the Holy Spirit. This is described throughout the book of Acts and is available to every believer.

Consider how the work of the Holy Spirit is so meticulously outlined throughout the entire book of Acts:

Acts 1	Promise: You shall receive power
Acts 2	Baptized with the Spirit in the Upper Room, speak in tongues
Acts 3	Lame man miraculously healed by the power of the Spirit
Acts 4	Holy Spirit infilling at prayer meeting

Acts 5	Ananias & Sapphira struck dead for lying to the Holy Spirit
Acts 6	Men full of the Holy Spirit chosen as deacons
Acts 7	The Jews resist the Holy Spirit
Acts 8	Samaritans baptized with the Holy Spirit
Acts 9	Saul converted and the church grows through the power of the Holy Spirit
Acts 10	The Gentiles baptized with the Spirit at Cornelius' house, speak in tongues
Acts 11	Holy Spirit warns of a coming world-wide famine
Acts 12	A Holy Ghost prayer meeting gets Peter delivered from jail
Acts 13	Holy Spirit separates Paul and Barnabas for missionary work (Paul's first missionary journey)
Acts 14	Lame man miraculously healed by the power of the Spirit
Acts 15	The Holy Spirit gives direction to the church
Acts 16	The Holy Spirit guides Paul (jail—earthquake—revival)
Acts 17	The Holy Spirit uses Paul on his second missionary journey to establish churches
Acts 18	The Holy Spirit uses Paul on his second missionary journey to establish churches
Acts 19	Believers at Ephesus baptized with the Spirit, speak in tongues
Acts 20	The Holy Spirit testifies in every city
Acts 21	The Holy Spirit warns Paul that persecution is coming
Acts 22-	The Holy Spirit helps Paul to navigate the

26	religious and political scene in Jerusalem and Caesarea
Acts 27	The Holy Spirit helps Paul in a shipwreck
Acts 28	Many on the island of Malta miraculously healed; Paul preaches at Rome by the power of the Spirit

God is not distant, but rather present in the person of the Holy Spirit. Over and over the New Testament describes the indwelling presence of God in the hearts of believers. In fact, 1 Corinthians 6:17 says, "He that is joined to the Lord is one spirit." The believer's spirit and the Lord's Spirit become one. The original Greek word for "joined" (*kollaó*) literally means "to be glued together."

In this glorious union, the Christian's spirit and the Holy Spirit become inseparable. In fact, Peter writes that we are "partakers of the divine nature" (1 Peter 1:4). No doubt, Peter's reference is in line with Paul's statement about being one spirit with the Lord. The average Christian, no doubt, lives well below ability and power bestowed.

Being God-inside-minded, puts the believer in the continuous mode of empowerment. Relegating God to an external Being is downgrading the effect of Christianity. The Christian who is God-inside-minded never has to ask, "Where are you God?"

The same power that raised Jesus from the dead, dwells in every believer.

Romans 8:9-11 (Message) But if God himself has taken up residence in your life, you can hardly be thinking more of yourself than of him. Anyone, of course, who has not welcomed this invisible but clearly present God, the Spirit of Christ, won't know what we're talking about. But for you who welcome him, in whom he dwells—even though you still experience all the limitations of sin—you yourself experience life on God's terms. It stands to reason, doesn't it, that if the alive-and-present God who raised Jesus from the dead moves into your life, he'll do the same thing in you that he did in Jesus, bringing you alive to himself? When God lives and breathes in you (and he does, as surely as he did in Jesus), you are delivered from that dead life. With his Spirit living in you, your body will be as alive as Christ's!

If God, indeed, has taken up residence within you, He will be the center of your thought life. We certainly have many limitations in our natural ability, but when we experience God's life on the terms of the Kingdom, we can accomplish anything.

Though the Kingdom is within, the results are demonstrated through our living.

1 Corinthians 4:20 (NLT) For the Kingdom of God is not just a lot of talk; it is living by God's power.

The King

Zechariah 9:9 Rejoice greatly, O daughter of Zion; shout, O daughter of Jerusalem: behold, thy King cometh unto thee...

In the book of Daniel, God gives His servant what is perhaps the most astounding prophecy in all of the Word of God. The book of Daniel was written in the 6th century B.C. We also know from secular history that the book was translated into Greek in 270 B.C. In chapter 9, Daniel was praying for the people of Israel, who were nearing the end of their Babylonian captivity. As he prayed, the angel Gabriel appeared to him and spoke the following words:

Daniel 9 (KJV)
24 Seventy weeks are determined upon thy people and upon thy holy city, to finish the transgression, and to make an end of sins, and to make reconciliation for iniquity, and to bring in everlasting righteousness, and to seal up the vision and prophecy, and to anoint the most Holy.
25 Know therefore and understand, that from the going forth of the commandment to restore and to build Jerusalem unto the Messiah the Prince shall be seven weeks, and threescore and two weeks: the street shall be

built again, and the wall, even in troublous times.

26 And after threescore and two weeks shall Messiah be cut off, but not for himself: and the people of the prince that shall come shall destroy the city and the sanctuary; and the end thereof shall be with a flood, and unto the end of the war desolations are determined.

27 And he shall confirm the covenant with many for one week: and in the midst of the week he shall cause the sacrifice and the oblation to cease, and for the overspreading of abominations he shall make it desolate, even until the consummation, and that determined shall be poured upon the desolate.

Israel had rebelled against God and as His chosen people. But God had a plan to make an end of their transgression, reconcile them to Him and bring them into everlasting righteousness. In doing so, He would seal up the vision and prophecy and anoint the Messiah, the King. Notice that this prophetic word was for "thy people" referring specifically to Israel. The prophetic timeline being referenced was not for the Church. However, the Church is greatly affected by the events of this prophecy.

To say that the words that follow verse 24 are amazing would be an understatement. Let's start with the very specific prediction in verse 25:

> **Daniel 9:25 Know therefore and understand, that from the going forth of the commandment to restore and to build Jerusalem unto the Messiah the Prince shall be seven weeks, and threescore and two weeks: the street shall be built again, and the wall, even in troublous times.**

A week of years equals 7 years. The Jewish and Babylonian calendars used a 360-day year. Therefore, 69 weeks of 360-day years totals **173,880 days**. In effect, Gabriel told Daniel that the interval between the commandment to rebuild Jerusalem until the presentation of the Messiah as King would be 173,880 days.

69 x 7 [week of years] = 483 [years]
483 x 360 [days per year] = 173,880 [days]

Prophecy teacher Chuck Missler has published detailed research to show precise dates of these events. His research was an enormous help in putting together this chapter. The commandment to restore and rebuild Jerusalem was given by Artaxerxes Longimanus on **March 14, 445 B.C.** We know this from the book of Nehemiah. In chapter 2 it states that the decree came down in the month of Nisan, which corresponds to our calendar months of March/April. The day of the month was not stated in Nehemiah; however, it was Hebrew tradition that if the specific day of the month was not given, then it meant the *first* of the month. The first day of the month Nisan was March 14th. We know what year it was because

23

Nehemiah 2:1 refers to the "twentieth year of the reign of Artaxerxes," which was 445 B.C.

For the second part of the prophecy in verse 25, the Word of God tells us exactly how the Messiah would be presented as King. Zechariah prophesied that the Messiah would present Himself as king by riding into Jerusalem on a donkey:

> **Zechariah 9:9 Rejoice greatly, O daughter of Zion; shout, O daughter of Jerusalem: behold, thy King cometh unto thee: he is just, and having salvation; lowly, and riding upon an ass, and upon a colt the foal of an ass.**

This is the only occasion that Jesus presented Himself as King. The date of this event was **April 6, 32 A.D.** The first Passover of Jesus' ministry would have been in the Spring of A.D. 29. The fourth Passover of His ministry was the day of his crucifixion and would have fallen in the year A.D. 32. According to the British Royal Observatory, the Sunday before that Passover was April 6th – the day that Jesus rode into Jerusalem on a donkey.

So here, in connection with Daniel's prophecy, we have two very specific dates. The first was the commandment to rebuild Jerusalem and the second was the presentation of the Messiah. Now, here is the astounding part: when we examine the period between March 14, 445 B.C. and April 6, 32 A.D., and correct for leap years, we discover that it is **173,880 days exactly!**

Can you fathom the greatness of God? Can you comprehend the precision in which the prophetic Word of God comes to pass? There is no way that Daniel could have known this in advance. The mathematical odds of such a precise prediction are too great to even number.

Before the Foundation of the World

> **Revelation 13:8 All who dwell on the earth will worship him, whose names have not been written in the Book of Life of the Lamb slain from the foundation of the world.**

> **1 Peter 1:20 He indeed was foreordained before the foundation of the world, but was manifest in these last times for you.**

Of course, the plan to send Jesus into the world to redeem mankind was not hatched in Daniel's day. Jesus was predetermined to be the Supreme Sacrifice by the foreknowledge of God. He knew that Adam would fail in the garden. The plan of God from eternity past was to come into the world as a man and take away the sin of the world.

Not only was Jesus foreordained to die on the Cross, but He also foreknew you and desires to have a personal relationship with you.

Highly Exalted

Philippians 2:5-11
5 Let this mind be in you which was also in Christ Jesus,
6 who, being in the form of God, did not consider it robbery to be equal with God,
7 but made Himself of no reputation, taking the form of a bondservant, and coming in the likeness of men.
8 And being found in appearance as a man, He humbled Himself and became obedient to the point of death, even the death of the cross.
9 Therefore God also has highly exalted Him and given Him the name which is above every name,
10 that at the name of Jesus every knee should bow, of those in heaven, and of those on earth, and of those under the earth,
11 and that every tongue should confess that Jesus Christ is Lord, to the glory of God the Father.

The Eternal Son, equal with the Father (v. 6), departed the throne of glory to be born of a virgin, conceived by the Holy Spirit, to be a man. Verse 6 tells us that He was in the *form* of God and verse 7 relays that He took on the *form* of a bondservant – i.e., a man. The same original word in the Greek is used for both. This word (*morphé*) means, "the figure, shape and inner essence." Jesus was fully God and fully Man. This is the miracle of the incarnation.

As God, Jesus temporarily laid aside the attributes of His deity – omniscience, omnipotence and omnipresence. He operated during His earthly ministry under the anointing of the Holy Spirit (Acts 10:38). This is seen in the Greek word (*kenoó*) translated "no reputation" in verse 7. The word literally means "empty out." This is theologically known as the *kenosis* of Christ – the temporary self-emptying of His divine attributes.

The King left His estate of eternal glory and became lower than the angels. "But we do see Jesus, who was made lower than the angels for a little while" (Hebrews 2:9). He was rich yet became poor in order to redeem fallen man.

> **2 Corinthians 8:9 For you know the grace of our Lord Jesus Christ, that though He was rich, yet for your sakes He became poor, that you through His poverty might become rich.**

The Cross

And being found in appearance as a man, He humbled Himself and became obedient to the point of death, even the death of the cross.

Jesus had one ultimate mission coming into the world – to suffer and die on the Cross for the sins of humanity. All of the Old Testament animal sacrifices were no more than types of the One Sacrifice that would take away the sin of the world. Hebrews 10:4

says that *it is not possible that the blood of bulls and of goats should take away sin.*

Further, the Law, which instituted the offering of sacrifices, was given to condemn the world of sin (Romans 3:19) – to reveal the need for a Savior.

Once a year on the Day of Atonement, the high priest entered the Holy of Holies with the blood of an animal sacrifice and placed it on the mercy seat covering the Ark of the Covenant. This was to provide atonement for sins of Israel for one year. However, the word *atonement* simply means "to cover." Their sins were never removed, only covered or bypassed due to the forbearance of God.

Only the blood of Jesus can remove the blight and stain of sin. He is the final and complete Atonement.

"It is Finished" (John 19:30)

The Name of Jesus

The Bible is clear that there is only one name whereby a person can be saved – the name of Jesus.

> **Acts 4:12 Nor is there salvation in any other, for there is no other name [Jesus Christ of Nazareth, v 10] under heaven given among men by which we must be saved.**

A name in the Bible is more than just a label. It signifies the nature and character of the person named. This is why many characters in the Bible had their names changed. This brief list is an example:

- Abram (high father) to Abraham (father of a multitude)
- Sarai (my princess) to Sarah (mother of nations)
- Jacob (supplanter) to Israel (having power with God)
- Simon (reed) to Peter (rock)

It should be understood that when we do something "in the name of Jesus," we are doing it in the character and nature of Jesus. Further, the name of Jesus represents authority. It has been given to the believer through the legal process of power of attorney. This means that a believer who is acting in the character and nature of Jesus may do all that Jesus would do if He were literally and personally present.

The Bible ascribes many names to Jesus. The list below is just 29 names out of more than 100 names of Jesus found in the Bible.

- Almighty (Revelation 1:8)
- Advocate (1 John 2:1)
- Alpha and Omega (Revelation 1:8)
- Amen (Revelation 3:14)
- Bread of Life (John 6:32)
- Captain of Salvation (Hebrews 2:10)
- Chief Shepherd (1 Peter 5:4)
- Holy One (Acts 3:14)

- I AM (John 8:58)
- Immanuel (Isaiah 7:14)
- Jesus
- King of Kings
- Lamb of God (John 1:29)
- Light of the World (John 8:12)
- Lion of the Tribe of Judah (Revelation 5:5)
- Lord of Lords (1 Timothy 6:15)
- Mediator (1 Timothy 2:5)
- Messiah (Daniel 9:25)
- Morning Star (Revelation 22:16)
- Only Begotten Son (John 1:18)
- Prince of Peace (Isaiah 9:6)
- Redeemer (Job 19:25)
- Resurrection and Life (John 11:25)
- Rock (1 Corinthians 10:4)
- Root of David (Revelation 22:16)
- Savior (Luke 2:11)
- Son of God (Matthew 2:15)
- True Vine (John 15:1)
- Word of God (Revelation 19:13)

Every Knee Will Bow & Every Tongue Confess

That at the name of Jesus every knee should bow, of those in heaven, and of those on earth, and of those under the earth, and that every tongue should confess that Jesus Christ is Lord, to the glory of God the Father.

The bowing of the knee signifies submission of one's will to the sovereign authority of the King. Every knee will ultimately bow to the name that is above every name. Some, those who belong to Him, will bow willingly and gladly, while others will bow from compulsion.

For those who adoringly bow out of worship, we have a "trailer," if you will, in Revelation chapter 4 when the *elders fall down before Him who sits on the throne and worship Him who lives forever and ever and cast their crowns before the throne, saying:*

> **"Holy, holy, holy,**
> **Lord God Almighty,**
> **Who was and is and is to come!"**

There are two main judgments to come:

1. The judgment of each believer's works to determine reward, known as the *Judgment Seat of Christ* (2 Corinthians 5:10).
2. The judgment of wicked at the end of the Millennium, known as the *Great White Throne Judgment* of God (Revelation 20:11-15). In this judgment all of the wicked dead will receive their final sentencing of eternity in the Lake of Fire.

In both of these judgments, every knee will bow and every tongue will confess the Lordship of Christ. For the second group, it will be too late to do so voluntarily.

Under His Feet

Ultimate dominion will come in the Millennial and Eternal Kingdom to come, but what about this present age? The writer to the Hebrews addresses this question in the second chapter of the epistle.

> **Hebrews 2:7-9**
> **7 You have made him a little lower than the angels; You have crowned him with glory and honor, and set him over the works of Your hands.**
> **8 You have put all things in subjection under his feet." For in that He put all in subjection under him, He left nothing that is not put under him. But now we do not yet see all things put under him.**
> **9 But we see Jesus, who was made a little lower than the angels, for the suffering of death crowned with glory and honor, that He, by the grace of God, might taste death for everyone.**

Verse 7 reiterates for us what we read in Philippians 2, that Jesus came as a man – a little lower than the angels, and was raised up and crowned with glory and honor. But verse 8 speaks to the present age and provides two contrasting perspectives:

1. All things are in subjection under His feet
2. But we do not <u>yet</u> see all things put under Him

This present age is temporal. Whenever a follower of Christ loses sight of that focal point, problems and adversity can become bigger than life. The Christian focus should be eternally-minded. The word *subjection* in the Greek (*hupotassó*) means, "to be under God's arrangement." God's arrangement for this dispensation is different than for the coming physical Kingdom. In the present, though we are redeemed, the earth is still under the curse of sin. Further, though our soul is redeemed, our bodies are still under the curse of sin – i.e., physical death.

This is, for lack of a better term, a probationary state. We are allowed to be tested and experience adversity due to the fallen world that we live in. God is preparing us for eternity through our life experiences as an overcomer. Please understand, the word probationary is not intended to convey that our salvation is still in question. Contrary, the Holy Spirit indwelling us is our guarantee of our eternal inheritance (Ephesians 1:14).

In the current economy of God, followers of Christ are in conflict with three enemies:

1. The Flesh (Romans 8:7; Matthew 26:41)
2. The World (James 4:4; 1 John 2:15)
3. The Devil (Ephesians 6:12; 1 Peter 5:8)

So while we do not *see* all things under His feet *yet*, we know that He is ultimately in control. The battles that we face as believers are not in vain. Though we see through a glass darkly and know in part, in the moment (1 Corinthians 13:12), there's coming a day when we shall see clearly and know in full. On that day, every tear will be wiped away.

> **Revelation 21:4 And God will wipe away every tear from their eyes; there shall be no more death, nor sorrow, nor crying. There shall be no more pain, for the former things have passed away.**

The King is Coming

The blessed hope of every believer is the second coming of Christ. That day is coming when Jesus will come back on a white horse, and we who've been raptured will ride back with him to take possession of the earth and initiate the physical kingdom of Christ.

> **Revelation 19:11-16**
> **11 Now I saw heaven opened, and behold, a white horse. And He who sat on him was called Faithful and True, and in righteousness He judges and makes war.**
> **12 His eyes were like a flame of fire, and on His head were many crowns. He had a name written that no one knew except Himself.**
> **13 He was clothed with a robe dipped in blood, and His name is called The Word of God.**
> **14 And the armies in heaven, clothed in fine linen, white and clean, followed Him on white horses.**

15 Now out of His mouth goes a sharp sword, that with it He should strike the nations. And He Himself will rule them with a rod of iron. He Himself treads the winepress of the fierceness and wrath of Almighty God.

16 And He has on His robe and on His thigh a name written:

KING OF KINGS ANDLORD OF LORDS.

The Kingdom & The Suffering Servant

John 1:1-3
**1 In the beginning was the Word, and the
Word was with God, and the Word was God.
2 He was in the beginning with God. 3 All
things were made through Him, and without
Him nothing was made that was made.**

"In the beginning." The other Gospels begin with
Bethlehem, but John starts with Eternity past. "In the
beginning" are also the very first words of the Bible
(Gen. 1:1). In the Hebrew, this is one word: *barasheet*
(ba-da-sheet)

The Hebrew language (OT) is beautiful, poetic and full
of mystery. There is an element to the language
known as pictographs. Each letter of the Hebrew
alphabet is assigned a specific pictographic symbol
and corresponding idea.

For example, this first word in the Bible - *barasheet*
(ba-da-sheet) conveys a beautiful message of the
Cross.

1. Bet – House or Tent
2. Resh – Head the first or highest person
3. Aleph – Ox or Bull "The first or ultimate
   strength of God"

4. Shin (Sheen) – Teeth "Destroy or Consume"
5. Yod (You'd) Arm (fist to elbow) "My hand, work or effort"
6. Tav – Cross "The Mark or the Covenant"

The first 2 letters, Bet & Resh, when put together (BAR) form the Hebrew/Aramaic word for "Son of" (e.g., Simon BarJonah).

- Bet + Resh = Son of (bar)
- Aleph = God, the first
- Shin (sheen) = to Destroy
- Yod (You'd) = By his effort or hand
- Tav = the Cross

"The Son of God will be destroyed (or killed) by His own hand (or effort) on a Cross"

> *The Lamb slain from the foundation of the world* (Revelation 13:8).

The Word

Jesus, here, is spoken of as The Word. This means He is the *"Personification of the revelation of God."*

> **Hebrews 1:3 (Berean) The Son is the radiance of God's glory and the exact representation of His nature, upholding all things by His powerful word.**

The Word was God

Jesus was not a created being; He is the Eternal Son of God, equal to the Father. This is why the Jews sought to kill Him. (1 Tim. 3:16 God was manifest in the flesh.)

> **John 5:17-18 "My Father has been working until now, and I have been working." Therefore the Jews sought to kill Him, because He not only broke the Sabbath, but also said that God was His Father, making Himself equal with God.**

v. 3) "All things were made by Him…"

He spoke the Universe into existence. He hung the earth upon nothing. He said, "Let there be light and there was light." In 6 days, He created the heavens (plural - the universe) and the earth and He rested on the 7th day.

The entire narrative of Genesis 1, God is referred to as *Elohim* ("The all-powerful One, Creator"), but in Genesis chapters two and three that describe God's personal relationship with man, He is called Yahweh – the covenant name of God. God desires personal relationship with man/woman, created in His own image.

One day, every knee will bow and every tongue will confess that Jesus is Lord (Phil. 2:10).

John 1:12, 14
12 But as many as received Him, to them He gave the right to become children of God, to those who believe in His name.
14 And the Word became flesh and dwelt among us, and we beheld His glory, the glory as of the only begotten of the Father, full of grace and truth.

Entrance into the Kingdom of God comes only through believing on His name. Not a mental assent – simply believing in His existence. To "receive" (*lambano*) means "to lay hold of." The word emphasizes the volition (will) and assertiveness of the receiver.

Jesus said, **"Unless one is born again he cannot see the kingdom of God"** in John 3:3.

> **v. 14) And the Word was made flesh, and dwelled among us, (and we beheld his glory, the glory as of the only begotten of the Father,) full of grace and truth.**

The Word (v. 1) was made flesh – The incarnation. Philippians 2 tells us that Jesus temporarily laid aside the attributes of His Deity and took on the nature of a man (Second Adam – Romans 5). He humbled Himself and became obedient unto the death of the Cross.

He was (and is) 100% God and 100% Man. 1 Timothy 2:5 "For there is one God, and there is one mediator between God and men, the man Christ Jesus."

The Kingdom of God is Not Religion

Romans 14:17 for the kingdom of God is not eating and drinking, but righteousness and peace and joy in the Holy Spirit.

Before we examine this verse, I want to clarify my usage of the word "religion." Religion is used in a positive way only once in the New Testament. James, in his letter, uses the phrase, "pure religion" to describe helping orphans and widows (James 1:26). Otherwise, there are two references to "the Jews religion" (Acts 26:5, Galatians 1:13-14). Religion is an outward observance to a written set of rules and code of conduct. It is most often accompanied with special ceremonies and rites. Christianity, on the other hand is about *relationship* with Jesus, not religious performance.

Now, onto Romans 14:17. The food and drink that Paul was referring to in this verse was in relation to religious and ceremonial observances. Should one or shouldn't one? Is it to be done this way or that way? Religion always gravitates toward the outward and manifests itself through rules. Jesus constantly came against this in His earthly ministry. It is pharisaical in nature.

The Bible actually does not condemn drinking wine, in moderation. However, the Scripture is clear in it's warning of strong alcohol. Of course, if a person has struggled with alcohol in the past, moderation would not be a good option. But the purpose of this section is not to debate wine drinking. That is a matter for every believer to personally resolve. The Bible tells us that if we cannot do something in faith, with a clear conscience, then it is sin (Romans 14:23).

Notice that the Kingdom qualities that are described in this verse are produced by the Holy Spirit – righteousness, peace and joy. The characteristics and attributes of the Kingdom of God cannot be duplicated by religion.

Righteousness: We are made to be the righteousness of God through the work of the Cross. There is nothing that we have done or could possibly ever do to earn this status of right standing with God.

> **2 Corinthians 5:21**
> **For He made Him who knew no sin to be sin for us, that we might become the righteousness of God in Him.**

Our righteousness is obtained through the sacrificial life of Jesus Christ. All of the Old Testament sacrifices were symbolic of the redemptive work of Christ. The five types of sacrifice below are explained in the book of Leviticus, chapters one through six.

1. **Burnt Offering:** The burnt offering was wholly consumed and symbolized that Jesus was completely obedient unto the death of the Cross. Philippians 2:8 says, "And being found in appearance as a man, He humbled Himself and became obedient to the point of death, even the death of the cross." Jesus was wholly consumed as our burnt offering.

2. **Sin Offering:** The sin offering was made when there was no possible restitution. The Law was given that the whole world might stand guilty of sin before God. There was no possible restitution that man could make. We were all condemned. Jesus took the sin of the whole world upon Himself, as 2 Corinthians 5:21 says. Jesus was made to be sin for us. This means that He was made to be the sin offering, not that he partook of the sin nature, as some have taught.

3. **Trespass Offering:** The trespass offering was made when restitution was required along with the animal sacrifice. As our trespass offering, Jesus made restitution with the Father on our behalf. We have been reconciled to the Father by the blood of Jesus! 2 Corinthians 5:19 says, "God was in Christ reconciling the world to Himself, not imputing their trespasses to them, and has committed to us the word of reconciliation."

4. **Peace Offering:** The peace offering was offered with the burnt offering. Parts of it were eaten by the priest and the worshipper. As believers, we share in His work on the Cross. Jesus said in John 6:54, "Whosoever eats my flesh, and drinks my blood, has eternal life; and I will raise him up at the last day." We are partakers of all the Jesus did on the Cross.

5. **Meal Offering:** The meal offering was a non-blood offering. It represents the earth-walk of Christ. For 33½ years, Jesus lived a perfect, sinless life. He was the Lamb of God without blemish. Hebrews 4:15 says, "He was in all points tempted as we are, yet without sin." Jesus was only able to offer His blood on the Cross because He had lived this perfect life without sin.

There is, of course, a counterfeit to true righteousness; it is called *self-righteousness*. The religious world is filled with people who are self-righteous. They boast of their good works and parade their piety before the eyes of men. But the Bible is clear on this very matter: *All of our righteousnesses are like filthy rags* (Isaiah 64:6).

Righteousness, therefore, is appropriated as a free gift from God. We are also called to *walk out* our righteousness as a witness to a sinful world. Jesus said, "I say to you, that unless your righteousness exceeds the righteousness of the scribes and Pharisees, you will by no means enter the kingdom of heaven" (Matthew 5:20). Clearly, the righteousness of the Pharisees was a derivative of their own religious works. As true believers, washed in the Blood, we have a righteousness that is genuine – a right standing with the Righteous Judge, Himself. Our lifestyles should reflect this standing.

Peace: God rules in our hearts by peace – Colossians 3:15.

> **And let the peace of God rule in your hearts, to which also you were called in one body; and be thankful.**

The original Greek word for "peace" in this verse (*brabeuó*) literally means "to umpire," as in an athletic event. An umpire makes the call when there is any dispute. He has the best vantage point and is trained to make those decisions. That's the way God's peace operates in our hearts.

As a local church pastor, I frequently warn my congregation: "Don't you dare do anything that resembles a major life decision without the peace of God in your heart." I would consider that to be my number one advice to any believer who's seeking the will of God. It doesn't matter what it looks like in the natural. If it appears that everything is falling into place but there's an absence of the peace of God in your heart, hold your ground. Wait until you have peace in your heart. Conversely, if you have God's peace that He is in something, it doesn't matter how bad it looks; trust in Him. Pretty much everything God has done in my life worked this way. He gave me a peace about it even though it looked impossible in the natural. As I trusted in Him and exercised my faith, the doors opened.

In God's Kingdom, peace is actually a much greater attribute than understanding.

> **Philippians 4:7 And the peace of God, which surpasses all understanding, will guard your hearts and minds through Christ Jesus.**

Understanding can only process what is known to the intellect. It must go through all sorts of filters such as logic and then try to find a frame of reference. Even then, it's faulty and unreliable. Peace, on the other hand, is instantaneous and intuitive in nature. Peace allows me to *know* something that I don't yet understand. In fact, I may never understand, yet I *know* through the function of God's peace in my heart.

Joy: The force of the Kingdom is joy. It is the unspeakable language of the Kingdom.

> **1 Peter 1:8 Whom [Jesus] having not seen you love. Though now you do not see Him, yet believing, you rejoice with joy inexpressible and full of glory.**

Kingdom joy is not dependent on the external circumstances of this life. There is sheer joy in knowing Him. Religion is often portrayed with downtrodden expressions in an effort to convey piety. But Christianity is a relationship that is rooted in joy.

Religion	Relationship
• Rules	• Life
• Performance	• Worship
• Ritual	• Spirit-filled
• Outward	• Inward
• Don't focused	• Do focused
• Pride	• Humility
• Works based	• Faith based
	• Joy

This joy of the Kingdom is not based on the works we do for the Lord, though there most certainly is joy in serving Him. Remember when Jesus sent the seventy out in Luke chapter 10? They came back with great joy because of the power that was demonstrated through them (v 17). Jesus reaffirmed that authority had indeed been given unto them, but then spoke these words.

Luke 10:20 Nevertheless do not rejoice in this, that the spirits are subject to you, but rather rejoice because your names are written in heaven.

In other words, don't rejoice because of the displays of Kingdom power, but instead know that your joy comes from being a Kingdom citizen. Our names are forever recorded in heaven. While it is always exciting to be used by God, true joy is a result of the abiding relationship that we have with the King of Kings.

The original Greek word for "inexpressible" used in 1 Peter 1:8 is *aneklalétos* and is used only here in the entire New Testament. Peter used this word to sum up the joy that he himself had experienced himself for over thirty years. It means "to which words are inadequate." Untold millions have experienced this same joy over the past two thousand years.

Thy Kingdom Come; Thy Will be Done

Matthew 6:10 Your kingdom come. Your will be done; on earth as it is in heaven.

The above verse is included in what is known as "The Lord's Prayer." Remember, the Greek word for "kingdom" is *basileia* and means, "The realm over which a sovereign exercises his authority." Our prayer, therefore, is that God will exercise His authority over every facet and detail of our life. This only comes through daily consecration and yielding to the Holy Spirit.

So many Christians are operating under the false premise that the *perfect* will of God is not necessary; that one may live in the "permissive" will of God and be blessed. This *permissive* will of God, as it is referred, is thought of as a *lite* version of God's will. The key feature being that I don't need to deny myself and follow Him, but instead pick and choose the parts I like. The false premise to this idea is that God has multiple choices or lite versions to His will for our lives. The reality of the situation is that God is permitting that person to have *his* or *her* will. This should not be confused with God's will. He wants the best for us, but will not impose on our freedom of choice.

We should be praying for God's will in our lives. But we should also understand that many areas of His will for us have already been revealed through His Word. A student of the Bible will understand that there are different types of prayer:

1. **Prayer of Faith:** (John 15:7; James 1:6-7) This is prayer that is in agreement with God's Word and its promises. It is never a matter of "If it be Thy will" when the Word explicitly reveals His will on the matter.

2. **Prayer of Agreement:** (Matthew 18:18-20) This type of prayer is when you join together with one ore more other believers to agree in prayer on a specific request.

3. **Prayer of Supplication:** (Philippians 4:6-7) Unlike the prayer of petition or intercession, which is praying on behalf of others, the prayer of supplication is generally a request for the person praying.

4. **Prayer of Intercession:** (Genesis 18; Philippians 1:19; Acts 12) Abraham's intercession for the people of Sodom is a great example of this type of prayer. Intercession is constant, fervent prayer on behalf of another or for a situation to change. Another example is in Acts chapter 12 when the church prayed persistently for Peter to be delivered and God sent an angel to deliver him from prison.

5. **Prayer of Praise & Worship:** (Psalms) This is the form of prayer that does not ask for

anything. It is seeking the Lord's face (His presence), not His hand (His acts).

6. **Prayer of Consecration:** (Luke 21:41-42) The sixth type, the prayer of consecration, is how one discovers the unique and individual components of God's will for his or her life.

When we seek God, He will reveal His will to enhance the explicit will of God that is disclosed in His Word. The unique will of God for our lives will never contradict or violate the explicit, written will of God in the Word.

The Kingdom assignment for your life is pre-ordained, before the foundations of the world.

> **Ephesians 2:10 For we are His workmanship, created in Christ Jesus for good works, which God prepared beforehand that we should walk in them.**

The original Greek word for "workmanship" (*poiema*) is the same root word that our English word *poem* comes from. Think about the structure of a poem; it often has unpredictable twists and unexpected turns. Yet in the nature of poetry, the author will bring everything into a beautiful ending. The same is true of a life that is yielded to God. The Lord will work all things together for good as we love Him through life's adventures.

Indicators

Your assignment is not a *decision*, but a *discovery*. Here are some indicators to your Kingdom assignment:

- **What do you love?** If someone claims to be called to the ministry of teaching but doesn't love to *study* the Bible, something is wrong.
- **What hurts you?** God allows us to go through suffering in life for a purpose. He always has a plan. I have found that those experiences were designed to birth in me a ministry to those who have been hurt or suffered in the same way, even if their situation is a little different (2 Corinthians 1:4).
- **What makes you angry?** Moses was angered when he saw the Israelites being mistreated (Exodus 2). His anger was an indicator to the assignment that God had given him.
- **What breaks your heart?** Ezra's heart was broken over the condition of the temple. This was God's way of assigning Ezra to the task of beautifying the temple (Ezra 7).

Geography

There is a *geographical aspect* of your Kingdom assignment. Consider Abraham (Canaan), Joseph (Egypt), Jonah (Nineveh) and Paul (Macedonia). All of these men were successful in their assignment, due in large part, to their obedience to the geographical aspect of their call. Of course, Jonah needed a little help.

Several years ago, I left my church in Indiana to take a pastorate in North Carolina. It was one of the worst decisions of my life, simply because God had not called me to North Carolina. I ignored the warnings from the Holy Spirit in my spirit and instead chose to focus on the outward signs that "appeared" to come together. It didn't end well, and ultimately, it took about two years to recover. But I learned a valuable lesson. You can't take a one-size-fits-all approach to *where* you complete your Kingdom assignment. Location matters.

An even bigger lesson learned was to never ignore the warnings of the Spirit. Generally speaking, I would describe it as *turbulence* in my spirit – the absence of peace. Remember the verse in Colossians that tells us to "let the peace of God rule in our hearts" (3:15). The Greek word for "rule" can also be translated as "umpire." It is an umpire's function to make decisions and rule on the play, safe or out. He is in the best position, up-close, to make the call. The same is true of the Holy Spirit; He knows the perfect will of the Father and wants to guide us in the way we should go. Our intellect and reasoning (as well as the circumstances) are much like the biased crowd at a distance that is not in position to make an accurate decision.

In another instance, during my first pastorate, I pastored a church in a very rural area. The church was growing and being blessed, but there were a certain segment of town's people who always said, "If you just moved into town, we would come." After a while, this began to make me feel that the church would always be limited if we stayed in that rural location. So we relocated to Main Street of this small town, and of course, none of the people who said they would come ever showed up. We got out of the will of God to please man. Even though it was only 10 miles up the road, we were never as blessed as we were in the rural location.

Most Christians are familiar with Paul's words in Philippians 3:13-14... forget the past... reach forth to the greater things in front of you... However, there is a key in verse 12 that unlocks this type of uncommon focus.

> **Philippians 3:12 Not as though I had already attained, either were already perfect: but I follow after, if that I may apprehend that for which also I am apprehended of Christ Jesus.**

Paul understood what he had been apprehended for – what his Kingdom assignment was. On the road to Damascus, when the Lord appeared to him, Paul prayed, "Lord, what do You want me to do?" (Acts 9:6). Shortly thereafter, Ananias received a word from the Lord for Paul: "He is a chosen vessel of Mine to bear My name before Gentiles, kings, and the children of Israel" (Acts 9:15).

No matter where you are at in your pursuit of the discovery of God's will, the following outline for God's will is always applicable, in any situation:

1. Rejoice always
2. Pray without ceasing
3. In everything give thanks

"For this is the will of God in Christ Jesus for you" (1 Thessalonians 5:16-18).

If you do these three things consistently (always, without ceasing, in everything), God will begin to unlock your Kingdom assignment within your heart.

Kingdom Thinking

Matthew 6:25, 31 (KJV)
25 Therefore I say unto you, Take no thought for your life, what ye shall eat, or what ye shall drink; nor yet for your body, what ye shall put on. Is not the life more than meat, and the body than raiment? 31 Therefore take no thought, saying, what shall we eat? or, what shall we drink? or, wherewithal shall we be clothed?

Those who are outside of the Kingdom are occupied with thinking about temporal needs. Jesus said, "For after all these things the Gentiles seek" (v 32). In other words, Jesus was saying that those outside of the covenant of God – i.e., the Gentiles, were consumed with meeting their external needs. This type of thinking amounts to little more than worry. But those who are in the Kingdom, in covenant with God, have no need to seek for their material or physical needs to be met.

Kingdom thinking is worry-free thinking. Notice that Jesus said, "Take no thought, saying..." This answers the question of *how* we "take" a thought. A thought is *taken* by speaking it out. Interestingly, the verb used (*merimnaó*) literally means "to be divided or distracted." When a Christian thinks and speaks negatively – worrying and anxious about physical needs, it causes a double-mindedness that produces failure. The Bible emphatically states that person won't receive anything from the Lord.

> **James 1:6-8**
> **6 But let him ask in faith, with no doubting, for he who doubts is like a wave of the sea driven and tossed by the wind.**
> **7 For let not that man suppose that he will receive anything from the Lord;**
> **8 he is a double-minded man, unstable in all his ways.**

The Bible also tells us to cast all our cares upon the Lord in 1 Peter 5:7. I love the way that the Amplified Bible translates this.

> **1 Peter 5:7 (AMP) Casting all your cares [all your anxieties, all your worries, and all your concerns, once and for all] on Him, for He cares about you [with deepest affection, and watches over you very carefully].**

Our anxieties, worries and concerns should be given to the Lord in prayer – once and for all! That means that we shouldn't be taking them back; to do so is to regress and fail to trust the Lord.

Renewing the Mind

Let me be clear on this matter: it is impossible to have Kingdom thinking without renewing the mind.

> **Romans 12:2 And do not be conformed to this world, but be transformed by the renewing of your mind, that you may prove what is that good and acceptable and perfect will of God.**

The word *conformed* means, "External patterns that don't come from within." We must stop following the external patterns that don't come from the *new man* inside. Remember, the Kingdom of God is within.

There are many Christians – genuinely born of God, who are living defeated lives. Much of it is due to a failure to renew the mind with God's Truth. Are any of the following traits at work in your life? If so, it's time to renew, or as the original word implies, renovate.

- Poor self-image
- Ungodly habits
- Destructive behavior patterns
- Rejection
- Fear
- Condemnation and guilt

Renewing the mind can be a lengthy process. In fact, it can take an entire lifetime in some cases. The good news is that there is improvement all along the way. But just when you think you've "got it all together," something triggers an area of your life that needs to be submitted to God. Kingdom thinking is not simply a destination but also a journey.

The Human Brain

There are two areas of the brain, in particular, we will focus on as it relates to renewing the mind.

- **The Limbic System**
- **The Prefrontal Cortex**

The Limbic System is the part of the brain that supplies instinct. Further, it is the emotional center of the brain. Emotions such as anger and pleasure are part of the Limbic System. Long-term memory is stored there. Most interesting, along with the memory, how we felt in that moment is stored and recalled as well. So when we are in similar situations, the mind will send out the same feelings as the original incident. The Limbic System is fully programmed by the age of six.

The Prefrontal Cortex, unlike the Limbic System, is not fully developed until the age of 25. This is the area of the brain that uses judgment, planning, and decision-making. Our moral code is developed in this part of the brain. It is where our emotional control resides.

In terms of behavior, the Limbic System is like the *gas pedal* that wants to act on impulse, without regard to good reasoning or moral code. The Prefrontal cortex, on the other hand, is like the *brakes* of the mind. It's not hard to see how this disparity can cause major problems. The adolescent in us wants to act out on impulse. But

God's Word tells us that we need to put away childish things.

> **1 Corinthians 13:11 When I was a child, I spoke as a child, I understood as a child, I thought as a child; but when I became a man, I put away childish things.**

The programming in our Limbic System needs to be renewed! It was programmed according to worldly patterns — external patterns that don't come from within.

The Limbic System	The Prefrontal Cortex
Complex system of nerves and networks in the brain (programmed by age 6) related to:	The cerebral cortex that covers the front part of the frontal lobe (not fully developed until age of 25).
• Instinct • Mood • Emotions • Fear • Pleasure • Anger • Drives (e.g., hunger, sex) • Long-term memory	• Judgment • Planning • Decision-making • Moral Code

The Limbic System, being wired to react impulsively, holds our long-term memories and the feelings that we had in those moments.

EXAMPLE:

A 35-year-old man, who had an earthly father that was verbally and physically abusive, comes to know the Lord at the age of thirty. However, he struggles in the area of trusting the Lord and believing in His love. He feels that when he fails, God is more than anxious to punish him.

This man must be renewed in the knowledge of God's perfect love. The Bible says, "perfect love casts out all fear" (1 John 4:18).

A true story example of this correlation is the life of Rich Mullins, the late Contemporary Christian Music artist of "Our God is an Awesome God" fame. I recently watched the movie based on his life story and Rich struggled terribly as an adult follower of Christ because of his relationship with his dad as a child. Though he loved God, he could never fully embrace God's love for him. He was greatly used by God and gave most of his lucrative earnings away to charity, but he never had the true inner peace that he longed for. Sadly, Rich was killed at the age of 41 in an automobile accident.

Many Christians suffer under the bondage of the past, never walking in the freedom that Christ provides. The mind goes unrenewed and destructive behavior patterns continue. True Kingdom living never happens because of the absence of Kingdom thinking.

The Spirit of our Mind

The New Testament also tells us to "be renewed in the spirit of our mind" (Ephesians 4:23). Below are some different translations:

New International Version
Be made new in the attitude of your minds.

New Living Translation
Instead, let the Spirit renew your thoughts and attitudes.

International Standard Version
Be renewed in your mental attitude.

Weymouth New Testament
Get yourselves renewed in the temper of your minds.

God wants us to be renewed in the attitude of our minds. Attitude is such a big part of the Kingdom lifestyle. What are some of the things that affect our attitudes?

- Relationships
- Music
- Television
- Social media
- Environments
- Stress – work and home
- Health

The Bible tells us to guard our hearts in Proverbs 4:23.

Guard your heart above all else, for it determines the course of your life. (NLT)

If you are not careful, it's easy to allow your mind to be conditioned to giving up. Statistics show that 90% of all first-time businesses fail, but 90% of all second-time businesses succeed. The problem is that 80% of people who fail the first time do not try again.

The Bible is filled with examples of leaders who failed the first time out, such as Joseph, Moses and Jonah. And others who wanted to quit along the way such as Elijah and Jeremiah. The key is that each of these men renewed their attitudes in the Lord and went on the great success.

Just because you have a limitation doesn't mean you can't reach your destination. Kingdom thinking is going to require some resilience and effort, but it is more than worth it in the end.

The Mind of Christ

Philippians 2:5 says, "Let this mind be in you that was also in Christ Jesus." Jesus had a Kingdom mindset. The Greek word for mind (*phroneo*) means "inner perspective." What this word is conveying is the idea of *the lens from which we view life*. God wants us to view life through the lens of His Kingdom. The preceding verse is the key to this Kingdom perspective.

> **Philippians 2:4 (ESV) Let each of you look not only to his own interests, but also to the interests of others.**

This is the mind, or *inner perspective* that was in Christ. He looked to the needs of others before His own. Kingdom living means seeing life differently than the world around us. The "prosperity gospel" is an affront to Kingdom living because its focus is on how you, the individual can be materially blessed and financially prosperous. This is opposite to the mind of Christ. That said, when a believer has the mind of Christ and puts others first, it is virtually impossible for that believer to be defeated.

Kingdom living requires some growing up and maturing in the Word to fully incorporate. In fact, if a follower of Christ remains in ignorance of God's truth, there will be much blessing that is forfeited.

> **Galatians 4:1 Now I say that the heir, as long as he is a child, does not differ at all from a slave, though he is master of all.**

"Child" (Gr. *nepios*) means "babe in ignorance." So even though every Christian has been called to live in the fullness of the Kingdom that is within them, the actual experience may be far below the bar. No matter where you stand today, make the commitment now to live out your remaining time on earth in the fullness of God's best for you.

Two Opposing Connections

Kingdom thinking is all about understanding the two different and opposing connections that are available to all believers. There is the connection with the world that is established through the flesh and there is the connection with God that is available via the spirit.

The flesh embodies "the old man" that has not been regenerated and will not be changed until the resurrection. This is the selfish orientation. The spirit is "the new man" and has been born again. The born again spirit is in communion with God and has the characteristics and fruit of the Holy Spirit.

The Flesh
Gr. Sarkos
"The Old Man - The Selfish Orientation"

Connection = World

- Pride
- Offenses
- Lust
- Jealousy
- Sensuality
- Idolatry
- Strife
- Anger
- Lust
- Self-Preservation

The Spirit
Gr. Pneuma
"The New Man"

Connection = God

- Love
- Joy
- Peace
- Longsuffering
- Kindness
- Goodness
- Faithfulness,
- Gentleness,
- Self-control

In order to live the victorious Kingdom life, the believer must become *spiritually minded*. It's been said that a person can be too spiritually minded for any earthly good, but that is opposite to what God's Word says. The truth is that people can be too earthly minded for any spiritual good.

> **Romans 8:5-8 (ESV)**
> **5 For those who live according to the flesh set their minds on the things of the flesh, but those who live according to the Spirit set their minds on the things of the Spirit.**
> **6 For to set the mind on the flesh is death, but to set the mind on the Spirit is life and peace.**
> **7 For the mind that is set on the flesh is hostile to God, for it does not submit to God's law; indeed, it cannot.**
> **8 Those who are in the flesh cannot please God.**

The instruction is to *set* our minds on the Spirit (v 6). Kingdom thinking is being spiritually minded.

Signs of the Kingdom

John 14:12 "Most assuredly, I say to you, he who believes in Me, the works that I do he will do also; and greater works than these he will do, because I go to My Father.

In the realm of God's Kingdom, the believers are supposed to do the same works that Jesus did. Below, I have set forth some remarkable facts about the ministry of Jesus.

Jesus did no miracles until He was baptized with the Holy Spirit and anointed by the Holy Spirit (Matthew 3:16-17, Luke 4:14). This means that Jesus lived on the earth for approximately thirty years before performing His first miracle. As He told His mother at Cana, his time had not yet come (John 2:4).

So many Christians have the idea that Jesus performed miracles because He was God – which He was, of course. But this is simply not what the Bible teaches. There is clear Scriptural evidence that when Jesus came to the earth, i.e., the incarnation, that He voluntarily laid aside the *attributes* of His deity.

While in the flesh, on earth, Jesus did *not* possess:

- Omnipresence

- Omniscience
- Omnipotence

Obviously, Jesus could not be everywhere at the same time (omnipresence). He limited Himself, as every other man, to being one place at one time. This was not the case in His pre-incarnate state in eternity past. Further, it is no longer the case in His resurrected state. Additionally, Jesus did not know all things (omniscience) during His earthly ministry. He knew only what was revealed to Him from the Father (John 5:19, 6:38, 8:28, 12:49-50, 14:10).

People often quote the words of Jesus from Mark 13:32 that the Son did not know the day and hour of His return, but only the Father. This is usually taken out of context to imply that Jesus still doesn't know when He's coming back. Jesus' reference was solely in regards to His humanity. In His glorified state, He has taken back up His omniscience. The Son knows all things, but in His humanity, He voluntarily and temporarily laid this aside in order to fulfill His mission.

Acts 10:38 tells us that the works and miracles that Jesus did were by the power of the Holy Spirit.

> **Acts 10:38 How God anointed Jesus of Nazareth with the Holy Spirit and with power, who went about doing good and healing all who were oppressed by the devil, for God was with Him.**

Where does it reveal that Jesus temporarily laid aside the attributes of His deity? Before answering the question, I must make clear that Jesus did not lay aside His deity, but the attributes or privileges of His deity. Jesus was, and is 100% God, while at the same time, 100% Man. This is the miracle of the incarnation. Now to the question of where the Bible communicates this truth:

> **Philippians 2:5-11**
> **5 Let this mind be in you which was also in Christ Jesus,**
> **6 who, being in the form of God, did not consider it robbery to be equal with God,**
> **7 but made Himself of no reputation, taking the form of a bondservant, and coming in the likeness of men.**
> **8 And being found in appearance as a man, He humbled Himself and became obedient to the point of death, even the death of the cross.**
> **9 Therefore God also has highly exalted Him and given Him the name which is above every name,**
> **10 that at the name of Jesus every knee should bow, of those in heaven, and of those on earth, and of those under the earth,**
> **11 and that every tongue should confess that Jesus Christ is Lord, to the glory of God the Father.**

Though Jesus was equal with God (v 6), He made Himself of no reputation. The Greek word for "no reputation" is *kenosis* and means, "to empty out, to deprive of content." Below are some other translations of this statement:

- He gave up his divine privileges (NLT)
- But emptied himself (ESV)
- But he stripped himself (Aramaic Bible in Plain English)

Therefore, understanding that Jesus did not perform His miracles through the function of being God, coupled with the fact that Jesus told His followers to do the same works (John 14:12), brings us to the conclusion that the signs and miracles of the Kingdom are for today and for each of His followers. The same Holy Spirit that raised Jesus from the dead dwells in each of us, if we belong to Him (Romans 8:11).

The Baptism with the Holy Spirit, as documented in the Book of Acts (2:4, 10:44-46, 19:2, 6), endues the believer with the power of God in order to do the works of Jesus – the signs of the Kingdom.

1 John 3:8 Jesus came to destroy the works of the devil.

Jesus, however, could do no mighty work or miracle in His hometown of Nazareth because of their unbelief (Mark 6). Those whom He grew up with committed the sin of familiarity.

Mark 6:3 Is this not the carpenter, the Son of Mary, and brother of James, Joses, Judas, and

Simon? And are not His sisters here with us?"
So they were offended at Him.

Verse five states, "Now He could do no mighty work there." Certainly, if Jesus was doing miracles by His sovereign will, He would not have been limited in Nazareth. This again testifies to the fact that Jesus was performing His ministry as a man anointed by the Holy Spirit.

Let's look at the healings and miracles of Jesus.

I find it interesting that eight of the 31 individual healings of Jesus included casting out demons (26%). So many today want to dismiss the notion that demonic activity is responsible for disease. But one of every four healings that Jesus performed testify that this is not the case.

> **Luke 11:20 But if I cast out demons with the finger of God, surely the kingdom of God has come upon you.**

The Kingdom of God is built upon the authority of the name of Jesus. To truly advance His kingdom, we must drive out demons.

In 11 cases, or 35% of the time, Jesus required a demonstration of faith before the healing occurred. While there has been much abuse and even plain nonsense associated with the subject of faith in recent years, we cannot throw out the baby with the bathwater. In other words, let us not ignore true

Biblical teaching simply because some carry it to extreme. There were times when Jesus healed without placing this requirement, but at least a third of the time Jesus only did what the faith of the person allowed Him to do.

The Kingdom of God has untold promises, but God has only obligated Himself to keep His conditional promises where they produce faith. Faith is the substance of things hoped for and the evidence of things not seen (Hebrews 11:1). I especially like the Amplified translation of that verse.

> **Hebrews 11:1 (AMP) Now faith is the assurance (title deed, confirmation) of things hoped for (divinely guaranteed), and the evidence of things not seen [the conviction of their reality—faith comprehends as fact what cannot be experienced by the physical senses].**

The Kingdom of God requires faith to accept as fact what cannot be experienced by the physical senses.

Additionally, in the miracles of Jesus we see group dynamic. Eight times, friends of the afflicted person assisted in the healing miracle. The Kingdom is all about helping one another reach our destinies in God. We can never reach our full potential without one another.

The Gospels are clear that signs and wonders, including physical healing, accompany the Kingdom of

God. These signs were not limited to the ministry of Jesus, Himself, but also to His followers.

> **Luke 9:2 He sent them to preach the kingdom of God and to heal the sick.**

> **Luke 10:9 And heal the sick there, and say to them, "The kingdom of God has come near to you."**

Further, signs were not limited to Jesus' followers of the first century. Those who hold a *cessationism* (i.e., the sign gifts have ceased) view should do a better review of church history. There were healings and miracles documented throughout the first several centuries of the church.

These are the last of the last days, spoken of by Joel (2:28) and preached by Peter on the day of Pentecost (Acts 2:17).   Jesus has spent two thousand years building the church and He's not coming back for something that is less than when He started. As in His first miracle, Jesus has saved His best wine for last!

The Kingdom Principle of Agreement

Matthew 18:18-20

18 Assuredly, I say to you, whatever you bind on earth will be bound in heaven, and whatever you loose on earth will be loosed in heaven.

19 Again I say to you that if two of you agree on earth concerning anything that they ask, it will be done for them by My Father in heaven.

20 For where two or three are gathered together in My name, I am there in the midst of them.

In this passage, Jesus is speaking to the church (v 17). We will connect the three verses together in order to understand how to bring the presence of God into our midst.

We must first understand the role and responsibility of the church in the earth. There was an Eternity Past and there will be an Eternity Future. Standing between the two is the present dispensation that we know as Time. God, in His sovereignty and providence, decided to create man in His own image and likeness (Genesis 1-2) and give him a free will. God gave this man dominion over the earth (Genesis 1:26).

Eternity Past		Eternity Future
	Time	

In this place called Time, God had voluntarily restricted Himself to what we, the church on earth, allows and forbids. God will not override the will of man and impose His will in this present dispensation. There is coming an Eternal Age, when every knee shall bow and every tongue confess that Jesus Christ is Lord (Philippians 2:10). But in this present time, God has allowed man to regulate His involvement.

Binding & Loosing

Therefore, we read that "Whatever we bind on earth will be bound in heaven, and whatever we loose on earth will be loosed in heaven." Earth *precedes* heaven. Interestingly, the tenses of the verbs bind and loose differ between earth's and heaven's. Earth's action is in the aorist tense, meaning a simple occurrence, while heaven's action is in the perfect tense – completed action in past time with present, continuous results. This is important to understand because God's will and word are forever settled in heaven (Psalm 119:89). God's will is completed action – before the foundations of the earth. But, He needs the church on earth to *release* His will and *forbid*, that, which contradicts His will.

Some synonyms of Bind and Loose:

> **Bind:** Restrict, Forbid, Disallow, Impede, Inhibit
> **Loose:** Release, Permit, Encourage, Develop, Unfasten

For the most part, binding and loosing has been looked on as little more than verbal declarations (most often spoken with a loud, authoritative voice). But there is so much more to what Jesus is saying. We cannot have a lifestyle that contradicts God's Word and yet bind or forbid the work of the enemy. Conversely, we cannot have a lifestyle that is in agreement with darkness and loose heaven's resources.

> **2 Corinthians 6:14-15**
> **14 Do not be unequally yoked together with unbelievers. For what fellowship has righteousness with lawlessness? And what communion has light with darkness?**
> **15 And what accord has Christ with Belial? Or what part has a believer with an unbeliever?**

The church has been assigned the task of managing heaven's resources. What are we doing with the resources God has entrusted us with? Isaiah 45:11 says, "Concerning the work of My hands, you command me." God has called us to pronounce the will of God in the earth. What we bind, heaven will bind for us on earth; whatever we loose, heaven will do likewise and release from heaven to earth.

Sadly, as Believers many have adopted the "It is what it is" mentality. But it is time to assume our God-given role in the earth. Jesus said, "We must work the works of him who sent me while it is day; night is coming, when no one can work" (John 9:4).

Prayer

> **Again I say to you that if two of you agree on earth concerning anything that they ask, it will be done for them by My Father in heaven.**

God places a numeric qualification on this matter of praying in agreement. There must be a minimum of two. This is so because He is addressing the church. The Greek word for "agree" is *sumphóneó*, meaning "symphony." A symphony must have harmony and accord. This is also a requirement for the prayer of agreement.

Understand, this type of agreement is not a simple matter of agreeing on a specific prayer request. The agreement requires goes much deeper and affects much more than the request. For the church to have the maximum output from prayer, she must be in agreement – in one accord. As two or more who "agree" we cannot have a spirit of disagreement or discord and simply agree on one matter of prayer. This is the root cause of many failed prayer requests. Discord and disagreement have permeated the ranks and yet we pray our recited prayers to no avail. God will not lower His condition for unity and agreement.

Within the community of local churches there is so much competition, jealousy and rivalry that the church has lost the ability to bind and loose and agree in prayer. We pray such small and limited prayers as a result. But we must learn that if we align with the instruction of verses 18 and 19, we cannot outpray heaven. God's resources in heaven are backed up and stacked up without the ability to be released in the earth because the church is not forbidding evil and releasing the power of the kingdom from a unified standing.

Obedience the absence of self-deceit in these matters will release heaven's resources upon the earth. What is self-deceit? James told us that if we are only hearers of the Word and not doers of the Word, we are deceiving ourselves (James 1:22). When Jesus saw Nathaniel, He said, "Behold and Israelite indeed, in whom is no deceit" (John 1:47). As a result, Jesus told him that he would see heaven open (v 50).

Through our disobedience, we close up heaven and its resources. We choose to trust in the arm of the flesh. If we have $1,000 and the Lord says to give it away and we don't, that's the most that $1,000 will ever be. But if we obey, that is the *least* that $1,000 will be. Because through obedience we unlocked heaven's resources.

What are the steps that need to be taken to release heaven's resources? Get in agreement with God's Word. Your lifestyle should reflect alignment with what God's Word agrees with and disagreement with what God's Word identifies as sin. Understand your authority in Christ. As a believer, it has been bestowed upon you to manage heaven's resources. Be a doer of the Word of God, not a hearer only.

Find a group that also agrees with God's Word and come into agreement with them. Do not stay in friendship with those who feed your weakness and minimize your role in the Kingdom. When David went to Israel's camp and pledged to take out Goliath, his brother Eliab met him and sought to minimize David and send him back to his father's house. But David turned away from him instead (1 Samuel 17).

Pray prayers of great power with faith in God. Know that the prayer of the church is God's outlet of power in the earth. The ministry of prayer within the church is the greatest source of power available on the earth today.

God's Presence

> **For where two or three are gathered together in My name, I am there in the midst of them.**

As God's people, we have been called to gather. Not to gather for just any purpose, but in His name, and for His name. God is building a temple, but unlike the Old Testament, it is not a physical structure made with human hands. This time, it is a spiritual temple made with living stones, shaped and fitted by the Holy Spirit.

> **1 Peter 2:5 You also, as living stones, are being built up a spiritual house.**

One interesting feature of the Temple of Solomon is that when it was built, the blocks were prepared or dressed at the quarry so that the sound of hammers, chisels and tools or iron would not be heard at the temple site.

> **1 Kings 6:7 And the temple, when it was being built, was built with stone finished at the quarry, so that no hammer or chisel *or* any iron tool was heard in the temple while it was being built.**

When we come together, we need to be prepared. We have heaven's business to conduct, not our own. Remember, these three verses are building and connecting, the one with the next.

- The church has been called to release God's power in the earth and to forbid the activity of Satan (v 18).
- The church has been called to come into a symphony of prayer. Not just little prayers for runny noses, but prayers that release heaven and move mountains. We are God's outlet in the earth (v 19).
- The church has been called to gather to lift up the name of Jesus (v 20).

Jesus tells us that when we gather in His name, that He is in our midst. In a strange way, this used to be one of my least favorite scriptures. I used it when hardly anyone showed up for church. With empty seats and a handful of people I would quote this verse to make myself feel better. But we weren't grasping the power of what Jesus was saying. He was talking about the church being described in verses 17 and 18 – one of authority, agreement and prayer. When that church comes together, even if two or three, the "I Am" is in our midst.

Where God's presence is in our midst and the focus is off ourselves and on Him, there will be great power on display. There will be healing, deliverance and salvation.

Heaven is backed up and stacked up with resources that Jesus Himself wants to deliver, but the church has forfeited its role of authority and squabbled over trivial earthly matters causing a serious condition of unanswered prayer and power shortage.

We are called to be meek, according to Matthew 5:5. Meek is not weak. In fact, the Greek word for meek (*pra-us*) is the word used for warhorses. To be meek is to "have great power that is under control of the Master." Jesus said that the meek would inherit the earth.

The Enemies of the Kingdom

1 Corinthians 2:8 Which none of the princes of this world knew: for had they known it, they would not have crucified the Lord of glory.

Satan played right into the hands of God when he conspired to crucify Jesus. What he thought was his greatest victory turned into his ultimate defeat three days later at the resurrection.

Now that Satan knows his time is short, he wants to thwart or hinder the work of the Kingdom as much as he can.

1 Peter 5:8 Be sober, be vigilant; because your adversary the devil walks about like a roaring lion, seeking whom he may devour.

The mindset of a Kingdom advancer must be sober (clear-headed) and vigilant (attentive or watchful). We cannot afford to be ignorant of the devil's devices (2 Corinthians 2:11).

The enemy will use the small areas of life to bring disruption, confusion, and failure.

Song of Solomon 2:15 The little foxes that spoil the vines.

If a person wants to change their destiny, it begins with changing their daily routine. Of course, Satan is our biggest enemy, but there are three enemies with which the believer must contend. These are encountered on a daily basis.

Enemies of the Kingdom:

- The world
- The flesh (selfish orientation)
- The devil

Jesus told us that although we are in the world, we are not of the world (John 17:16). As we discussed in the chapter on Kingdom Thinking, our minds must be renewed away from conformity to the world's ways.

The flesh, or selfish orientation is what we deal with on a daily basis. Unless we maintain discipline over the flesh, we will live inconsistent lives. Even someone as spiritual as the apostle Paul understood the propensity of the flesh to bring ruin.

1 Corinthians 9:27 But I discipline my body and bring it into subjection, lest, when I have preached to others, I myself should become disqualified.

As a pastor, I like to remind people that I may have a gift and an anointing to teach and preach the Word of

God, but I don't have any special ability to live out the Word more than any other believer. This is, in essence, what Paul is telling the Corinthians. It is a shame that some very large ministries have been brought down by sexual sin and immorality. It has been said that one can lose in 20 minutes what took 20 years to build.

Of course, the devil uses the flesh's tendencies to entrap people into sin and destructive behavior. The sixth chapter of Ephesians deals with this struggle.

> **Ephesians 6:11-12**
> **11 Put on the whole armor of God, that you may be able to stand against the wiles of the devil.**
> **12 For we do not wrestle against flesh and blood, but against principalities, against powers, against the rulers of the darkness of this age, against spiritual hosts of wickedness in the heavenly places.**

Wrestling, unlike other word choices for fighting, always includes *physical contact*. Many are ignorant of the fact that people are in contact combat with Satan's cohorts on a regular basis. Paul himself said that he was "buffeted" by the messenger of Satan (2 Corinthians 12:7). The Greek word for buffet literally means, "to strike with the fist." Paul understood the nature of his conflict.

Further, as verse 12 indicates, because Satan is not omnipresent, he has a hierarchy of demonic spirits within his organization.

1. **Principalities** (Gr. *arché*): These are the highest-ranking demons, or arch (fallen) angels. *Arché* means "first in order." From a military perspective, these would be considered Generals. Principalities rule over nations, like the "Prince of Persia" in Daniel chapter 10.

2. **Powers** (Gr. *exousia*): These are lesser in rank than principalities, but still "officers" in Satan's army. *Exousia* actually means "authority." These demons are high up in rank, with authority over lower level demons. When a person yields their life to these authorities, murder, rape and all sorts of human destruction are the result.

3. **Rulers of Darkness** (*kosmokratór*): These demons are likely the promoters of spiritual darkness – e.g., false religion and the occult. Satan's goal is to blind the minds of people and keep them in spiritual darkness (2 Corinthians 4:4).

   2 Corinthians 4:4 Whose minds the god of this age has blinded, who do not believe, lest the light of the gospel of the glory of Christ, who is the image of God, should shine on them.

4. **Wicked Spirits** (*ponéria*): These lowest level demons operate in the daily affairs of humans to tempt and ensnare them.

We must dress in the whole armor of God in order to overcome Satan's wiles.

1. **The Belt of Truth** (v 14): The Roman soldier's belt was large with many loops to hold weapons (the Lord has many weapons available for the Spirit-filled believer). It was tied in several places to keep it secure (all of God's truth must be appropriated). Further, there were markings to designate past campaigns (we are overcomers).

   Truth and integrity of heart is what holds the armor together. When one departs from God's truth and personal integrity all else is out of place.

   Jesus said that it was the Truth that we know that would make us free (John 8:31-32). The Believer's armor must be held together by revelation truth from God's Word.

2. **Breastplate of Righteousness** (v 14): The breastplate was connected to the belt. It was not clunky but lightweight enough to allow freedom of movement. Conversely, the righteousness of God doesn't weigh us down. The Pharisees had 613 laws and thousands of traditions that they had made up. Talk about

being weighed down! However, the Bible says in 1 John 5:3 that God's commandments are not burdensome.

The breastplate covers the vital organs such as the heart. It is the righteousness of God in Christ that covers us. All of our righteousness is as filthy rags. His righteousness must be go beyond a legal fact to an experiential reality in our lives if true protection is to be found.

Satan attacks the Believer's right standing with God probably more than any other area. He tries to place a blanket of guilt upon us to get us to draw back from God. Righteousness produces boldness!

3. **Gospel Shoes** (v 15): The Roman soldier's shoes were heavy-soled sandals with metal studs on the bottom for good footing on uneven or slippery ground.

The center of the believer's life must be focused on evangelism. This puts our attention and concerns on the needs of others. When our focus is self-centered in our Christian walk, there is a hole in the armor.

Shoes reflect one's walk. The Believer's walk must be about more than individual needs. Get involved in the work of the ministry – put your gospel shoes to work!

4. **Shield of Faith** (v 16): The Roman soldier's shield was long and rectangular (knees to chin). When they had an arrow barrage, they would get on their knees for protection. Similarly, the believer must get on his knees in prayer during times of attack.

   Faith quenches all of the fiery darts of the wicked one. When Satan was attacking Simon Peter, it was Peter's faith that Jesus prayed for (Luke 22:31-32). It is the faith of God in our hearts that overcomes the world (I John 5:4). Faith comes by hearing and hearing the Word of God (Romans 10:17).

   One of the reasons that God allows Satan to continue is to allow our faith to be developed. Faith comes by hearing the Word, but it is exercised when we go through the circumstances of life.

   One additional comment about the shield: soldiers could also come together when under attack and hold their shields over their heads, side by side, and provide a covering – a canopy of protection. Remember, the shield is not only for your protection, but also for the body.

5. **Helmet of Salvation** (v 17): The Roman soldier's helmet was the best helmet in the ancient world. It provided total protection in the head area.

Since the helmet covers the head area, it should be understood that this represents the mind. The importance of protecting the thought life cannot be emphasized enough. Here once again it is reiterated to us that we need to cover our minds with God's armor. More often than not this is the place that Satan finds access.

Two areas of our thought life that Satan wants to control:

- The *memory* to replay the past
- The *imagination* to pre-play the future

6. **Sword of the Spirit (Word of God)** (v 17): This is the only offensive weapon in our arsenal. "Word" here is the Greek word *rhema*, meaning "the intimate personal word from God as spoken through His overall Word." In other words, it is not *head* knowledge of the Word that will defeat the devil. It is the revelation knowledge of the Word spoken out of our mouths from the spirit that will drive back the enemy. This is the weapon that Jesus Himself employed during His, wilderness temptation. Three times Jesus declared "IT IS WRITTEN!" until Satan had to flee!

Satan knows the written Word, but he has no revelation knowledge of the Truth because he is cut off from the life of God.

Roman soldiers were taught to thrust, not cut. A stroke with the edge rarely kills, but a stab is usually fatal. The *rhema* of God is like a pinpoint stab into Satan's unprotected area.

7. **Prayer** (vv 18-19): This is not a weapon per say, but the place in which the weapons are engaged. The armor is not a metaphor without any practical value. The armor is dynamic in its working when employed in prayer. This is the battleground, where the battle is fought and won. Satan trembles when the weakest saint of God gets on his knees to pray. Satan is not fearful of men of *standing*, but rather men of *kneeling*.

Kingdom Authority

As discussed in the chapter on Agreement, believers have the authority to bind and to loose the resources of the Kingdom of Heaven.

> **Matthew 18:19 And I will give you the keys of the kingdom of heaven, and whatever you bind on earth will be bound in heaven, and whatever you loose on earth will be loosed in heaven.**

Kingdom authority does not come from a title or earthly status. So many of God's people are jockeying for position, but humility is the key is the promotion that comes from God. Even the disciples – James and John wanted to sit at the right and left sides of Jesus in glory (Mark 10:37). On the night of the last supper, the twelve were arguing among themselves which one would be the greatest (Luke 22:24). Here is the response of Jesus:

> **Luke 22:25-26**
> **25 And He said to them, "The kings of the Gentiles exercise lordship over them, and those who exercise authority over them are called 'benefactors.'**
> **26 But not so among you; on the contrary, he who is greatest among you, let him be as the younger, and he who governs as he who serves."**

The kings of the Gentiles were called benefactors by the court flatterers who were doing so to conceal the cruelty and tyranny of the rulers. However, God's ways are *contrary* to the world's. Jesus said that the one who governs or leads should be as one who serves. Thus, Kingdom authority is transmitted by the act of serving.

Further, it must be understood that Kingdom authority is spiritual and not worldly in nature. Jesus said, "My Kingdom is not of this world" (John 18:36). Please remember that when man was created, he was given authority from God.

> **Genesis 1:27-28**
> **27 So God created man in His own image; in the image of God He created him; male and female He created them.**
> **28 Then God blessed them, and God said to them, "Be fruitful and multiply; fill the earth and subdue it; have dominion over the fish of the sea, over the birds of the air, and over every living thing that moves on the earth."**

The Hebrew word for "dominion" (*radah*) means "to rule, to dominate, to prevail against." Man forfeited this authority in the garden when he rebelled against God. However, what the first Adam lost at the tree of the knowledge of good and evil, the Second Adam won back at the tree on Calvary (Romans 5:12; 1 Corinthians 15:22, 45). In Christ, the believer has authority.

Power vs. Authority

There is a difference between power and authority. We see both of the words in play in Luke 10:19, when the seventy returned from their ministry trips.

> **Luke 10:19 Behold, I give you the <u>authority</u> to trample on serpents and scorpions, and over all the <u>power</u> of the enemy, and nothing shall by any means hurt you.**

The Greek word for *power* used here is *dunamis* and means "the ability to perform." When used of believers it is used in connection with the Holy Spirit who lives in us. It is His power that resides in us and gives us the ability to perform God's work in the earth. However, in this verse, it is the *power of the devil* being referenced. More on that in a moment. The Greek word for *authority* is *exousia* and means "to be authorized to rule within a jurisdiction."

Prior to the Cross, Satan had legal right to dominate over man. It was given to him through man's disobedience. However, the Bible declares that Satan has been disarmed of his authority through the Cross (Colossians 2:14-15). But the devil still has *power* – ability to perform evil. Nevertheless, the believer has *authority* over the devil – *exousia*, the authority to overrule Satan's power within the jurisdiction of our lives that are bought by the Blood.

The devil can never outright *overpower* the believer. There must be deceits involved. Scripture after Scripture warns us of the devil's wiles.

> **Ephesians 6:11 Put on the whole armor of God, that you may be able to stand against the wiles of the devil.**

> **John 8:44 You are of your father the devil, and the desires of your father you want to do. He was a murderer from the beginning, and does not stand in the truth, because there is no truth in him. When he speaks a lie, he speaks from his own resources, for he is a liar and the father of it.**

> **John 10:10 The thief does not come except to steal, and to kill, and to destroy. I have come that they may have life, and that they may have it more abundantly.**

> **2 Corinthians 2:11 Lest Satan should take advantage of us; for we are not ignorant of his devices.**

Repeatedly, the Bible warns us against the manipulation of the devil. Satan cannot steal, kill and destroy the believer by the force of his own will and power. Instead, the enemy will conspire, deceive, plot and manipulate in order to convince us to yield our authority to his power.

Believers must stand strong in faith and resist the devil. Too often, Christians try to resist the devil without first submitting to God. James 4:7 clearly states the order:

1. Submit yourself to God
2. Resist the devil

Under these orders, the devil "will flee from you."

Power of Attorney

The authority of the Kingdom is accomplished through the name of Jesus. The Bible says that every knee must bow to His name (Philippians 2:10-11). But what does it mean to do something "in the name of Jesus?" Christians throw around "in the name of Jesus" at the end of every prayer, but very little prayer is getting answered.

First off, in Bible times a name meant something more than a label by which to call something or someone. It spoke of the character and nature of that person. Thus we have several examples in the Bible of names being changed as a result of a change of character (e.g., Jacob to Israel). Therefore, we shouldn't pronounce the name of Jesus in a manner than conflicts with His nature and character. In other words, what would Jesus do if He were personally present? His character and nature are explicitly revealed in the Gospels.

Secondly, to act in one's name was the equivalent of the power of attorney. Simply stated, this means to act on one's behalf, as their authorized representative, as the authorizing party would do if he or she were personally present. The power of attorney carries full legal right to act on the behalf of the other, within the prescribed jurisdiction.

Therefore, let us answer the question, "What does it mean to do something in Jesus' name?" It means to act as Jesus' authorized representative and do and perform all that He would do if He were physically and personally present. Further, it limits these actions to works that fit within His personal character and nature. If greed is the motivating factor of what I'm praying for, it falls outside of the character of Jesus. But if I'm asking in alignment with His character and agreement with His Word, and have faith in my heart, there is nothing impossible.

> **John 14:12 Most assuredly, I say to you, he who believes in Me, the works that I do he will do also; and greater works than these he will do, because I go to My Father.**

The Kingdom Anointing

Jesus & The Anointing

At the age of 30, Jesus entered His public ministry by being baptized by John the Baptist. At that point, the Holy Spirit descended upon Him like a dove.

> **Matthew 3:16 When He had been baptized, Jesus came up immediately from the water; and behold, the heavens were opened to Him, and He saw the Spirit of God descending like a dove and alighting upon Him.**

It is interesting that a dove has nine main feathers in its right wing and nine main feathers in its left wing. There are nine gifts of the Spirit (1 Corinthians 12) and nine fruits of the Spirit (Galatians 5). Further, a dove has five main feathers in its tail. There are five ministry gifts (Ephesians 4). Our Lord walked in the fullness of the gifts of the Spirit, the fruit of the Spirit and the ministry gifts.

Upon being baptized with the Spirit and subsequently tested, Jesus entered His hometown to announce His ministry. He went into His home synagogue in Nazareth and began to read from the book of Isaiah (chapter 61).

Luke 4:18-19
18 "The Spirit of the Lord is upon Me, because He has anointed Me to preach the gospel to the poor; He has sent Me to heal the brokenhearted, to proclaim liberty to the captives and recovery of sight to the blind, to set at liberty those who are oppressed;
19 To proclaim the acceptable year of the Lord.

Jesus told the people that He was the fulfillment of this prophecy (v. 21). Instead of rejoicing, the people were filled with wrath and tried to push him over a cliff (vv. 28-29). Everyone is not excited about the anointing. Religion wants to stifle the anointing because it takes the control and the glory away from man.

There was a five-fold purpose for the anointing of the Holy Spirit upon Jesus.

     a.   Healing for the brokenhearted
     b.   Liberty to the captives
     c.   Recovery of sight to the blind
     d.   Liberty to the oppressed
     e.   Acceptable Year of the Lord

Wherever Jesus went, He operated as a man anointed with the Holy Spirit and power, destroying the works of the devil.

Acts 10:38 How God anointed Jesus of Nazareth with the Holy Spirit and with power, who went about doing good and healing all who were oppressed by the devil, for God was with Him.

The anointing of the Holy Spirit was the evidence that the Kingdom of God had come.

Matthew 12:28 But if I cast out demons by the Spirit of God, surely the kingdom of God has come upon you.

When Jesus came to the earth, He temporarily laid aside the attributes of His deity. Jesus was and is 100% God and, at the same time, 100% man. Jesus did all of His miracles, while on the earth, by the anointing of the Holy Spirit (Acts 10:38). Jesus never fit the religious mold and often did things deemed peculiar when ministering to people.

The Kingdom of God does not fit the paradigm of man. The anointing will often lead you to do things that human logic rejects because it doesn't "fit into the box."

Unbelief

As mighty as the ministry of Jesus was, He could not overcome the unbelief of those who rejected His Word. The anointing upon Jesus was subject to the reception of the people. In Mark's gospel, it was written that Jesus could do no mighty work in His own hometown because of unbelief (Mark 6:1-6).

> **Mark 6:5-6**
> **5 Now He could do no mighty work there, except that He laid His hands on a few sick people and healed them.**
> **6 And He marveled because of their unbelief.**

Diversity

In 1 Corinthians 12, the Bible discusses the supernatural gifts of the Holy Spirit. In that passage, there are two words that are used in tandem that in every other context would be antonyms – opposites. But when the supernatural operation of the Holy Spirit is involved, they flow together!

> **1 Corinthians 12:4-6**
> **4 There are <u>diversities</u> of gifts, but the <u>same</u> Spirit.**
> **5 There are <u>differences</u> of ministries, but the <u>same</u> Lord.**
> **6 And there are <u>diversities</u> of activities, but it is the <u>same</u> God who works all in all.**

These two words are *diversities/differences* and *same*. Diversity and Sameness will flow at the same time when the anointing is present. In other words, we all function a little differently (diversity), but it's the same Holy Spirit that is anointing us. Don't try to copy other people. Function in the unction that God has given you.

The Kingdom of God can only be advanced when people are operating in the anointing and the anointing is individual with each person. In this same passage where Paul lists nine supernatural gifts of the Spirit, he also uses an analogy of the human body to describe the church. He says that *God has set the members, each one of them, in the body just as He pleased. And if they were all one member, where would the body be (vv 18-19)?* We are many members but one body.

It's all about finding your place in the Kingdom and learning how to flow in the anointing of the Spirit. The anointing is the *dunamis* power of God – the very presence that Jesus told the disciples to wait for before they began their ministries (Luke 24:49). I wouldn't dare attempt to do anything for God without the anointing of the Holy Spirit.

Throughout Scripture, oil is a symbol of the Holy Spirit and the anointing. In Ezekiel 44, instructions for Levites while in the inner court of the Temple are given. Verse 18 says that they shall not wear any garment that causes them to sweat or perspire. The message is that God cannot use the energy of the flesh to accomplish what only the Spirit can do. The sweat of the flesh is a counterfeit to the oil of the Spirit. Sweat was a byproduct of the fall of man (Genesis 3:19) and represented that man now toiled apart from God. There is too much ministry today, in God's house that is performed by the sweat of the flesh, under the absence of the Spirit.

Other than these two passages in Ezekiel 44 and Genesis 3, sweat is only mentioned one other time in Scripture – in the garden of Gethsemane as Jesus prepared for the Cross. When considering the three occasions, it's a beautiful connection.

1. Sweat represented the curse of working apart from God.
2. Jesus sweat great drops of blood and went to the Cross to restore us to God.
3. We now enter God's presence by grace and without the sweat of our efforts.

Sweat = separation from God, our talent, intellect and pride

Oil = the anointing of the Spirit, gifting and humility

What is the Anointing?

In 33 years of serving God, I've never heard a really good definition of the Holy Spirit. Why is it so hard to qualify and define? If it could be easily defined, man would simply try to duplicate it. And make no mistake, people have tried since the days of the Book of Acts, but they always fall flat.

The Kingdom of God is the penetration of heaven into the physical realm. The conduit from which this force flows is the anointing within – where the Kingdom of God dwells (Luke 17:21). Jesus prayed the following (Matthew 6:10):

Your kingdom come.
Your will be done
On earth as it is in heaven.

The original Greek word for "be done" is *ginomai* and means, "to emerge, to become, to come into manifestation." True spiritual work that is done – work that has eternal value – is brought about through the anointing of the Holy Spirit. When the Holy Spirit comes into manifestation through a person, it is apparent. It is not to be confused with personal charisma. The Kingdom of God cannot be advanced with the personality of man. All this will do is establish personal kingdoms that will be brought down by God.

How to Learn to Walk in the Anointing

The Bible teaches that the anointing is *within* us. It is important to make the connection: Jesus said that the Kingdom of God is within us (Luke 17:21) and the Bible goes on to say that the anointing of God is within us.

> **1 John 2:20, 27**
> **20 But you have an anointing from the Holy One, and you know all things.**
> **27 But the anointing which you have received from Him abides in you, and you do not need that anyone teach you; but as the same anointing teaches you concerning all things, and is true, and is not a lie, and just as it has taught you, you will abide in Him.**

Once more, the role of the Holy Spirit is seen as Teacher in this passage. How does the Holy Spirit teach us? There are three primary ways that the Holy Spirit teaches God's people:

1. Revelation from studying the Word of God
2. Truth that comes from anointed teachers
3. Experiences of a Spirit-led life

The third one, experiential learning, comes from being a doer of the Word of God (James 1:22). As you practice the Word and apply it in your life, you gain the experience and knowledge of walking in the anointing. There are some things that can only be learned from practical experience.

The anointing doesn't make you better than anyone else; it makes you *more than* you. It is the energy (Gr. *energia*) of the Holy Spirit working through you. For example, in church when the Holy Spirit is moving during an altar call, the anointing is present to touch people. If I am praying for people at that time, my prayers will be more effective than if you stop by my office on Tuesday morning. It isn't that God won't answer my prayers on Tuesday, but when the anointing is present, there is more immediacy of the Kingdom of Heaven emerging into the earthly realm.

Kingdom Connection

Con·nect

kəˈnekt/

verb

- Bring together or into contact so that a real or notional link is established.
- Join together so as to provide access and communication.
- Link to a power supply.

A couple of things stand out to me when looking at the definition of *connect*. First, the link that is established can be either *real* or *notional*. Notional means to *exist only in theory*. Secondly, a connection is frequently used to link to a power supply. Both of these meanings have application to the concept of a Kingdom connection.

I have researched the subject of *Church and the Millennials*. Millennials are the generation that was born from the early 80's through 2000. How can the church reach them? What makes them different from previous generations? There were two basic realities that stood out to me in my research:

1. Millennials are looking to connect with a group.
2. Millennials are looking for something authentic and real.

If the church is going to advance the gospel of the Kingdom to this generation, we have to, somehow, establish a connection with them. Just providing shallow linking to the culture of today with the gospel is not enough. The apostle Paul plainly said that *he became all things to all people, that by all means he might save some* (1 Corinthians 9:22).

What did Paul mean when he said that he "became all things?" Should the church learn pop culture and mimic the current trends of society within the church? No! That isn't what Paul is referring to. First we must understand how the gospel interacts with culture.

There are some very strong Biblical examples about prophets, preachers and leaders being culturally relevant. Here are a few:

Jeremiah: God brought this prophet into the world at a specific time in Israel's history, called from his mother's womb (1:5) to reach the people of his generation who were going into captivity. Culturally relevant doesn't always mean popular. But in the end, Jeremiah's message was one of healing and restoration (29:11).

Esther: This woman of God helped save a nation. She was placed into position as Queen in order to preserve the Jewish race. Esther outwitted Haman, who wanted to destroy God's people. She knew that she couldn't be silent and do nothing. She understood that she had attained her royalty "for such a time as this" (4:14).

John the Baptist: John was the forerunner of the Messiah. He knew his time and his purpose. "Prepare the way for the Lord, make straight paths for him" (Mark 1:3). He cried out to a generation that had become wicked to repent (Matthew 3:1-2). John didn't try to conform to the religious norm of his day, with either his appearance or his message.

These three people were world-changers. They had specific assignments from God that were relevant to the people of their generation. The Holy Spirit has something to say to this generation and He wants to use the church to deliver the message. If we are cutting off our audience with antiquated methodologies, what are we really accomplishing in the name of the Lord? Too often, churches are simply holding down the fort, and sometimes even doing a poor job of that.

One of the most important Kingdom principles to learn is that God wired His people to change, adapt and overcome. But people fear change. The idea of painting the church ceiling or replacing an altar sends shock waves through the faithful. We don't need change for the sake of change (although sometimes that's not bad), but we need to be change agents in order to advance the Kingdom in an ever-changing world around us.

The NLT renders 1 Corinthians 9:22 this way: *I try to find common ground with everyone, doing everything I can to save some.* This does not mean that we become like the world, but instead find common ground with the people we are trying to reach. Recently, I heard a radio interview with a woman who was formerly a lesbian before coming to Christ. She was a college professor and a leader in the LGBT community. Today, she is a pastor's wife – praise God! But she made an interesting comment, she said, "Too often, Christians use the Bible like a punctuation mark to end a conversation instead of using it to engage the unbeliever in a conversation to lead them to Christ." In other words, just declaring, "The Bible says…" and then walking away. This is talking *at* people and not *with* them. Jesus always engaged people. He could tie the gospel to anything, from a fishing net to a bucket of water. This helped people connect to the message of the Gospel.

The Bible could not be more relevant to the problems of society today, but the problem occurs when it's preached in an irrelevant way, with a focus more on form than substance. Jesus said to the religious people of His day, "You cancel the Word of God in order to hand down your own tradition" (Mark 7:13 NLT).

When trying to connect people with the Kingdom, we must bear in mind that people no longer attend church simply because it's the right and moral thing to do. Further, people no longer attend church due to societal pressure from the community. These were the case a couple of generations ago, but no longer today. Today, unless there is a compelling reason to do so, people will do almost anything other than go to church. It is the mission of the church to give them that compelling reason.

> **Luke 14:23 (NASB) Go out into the highways and along the hedges, and compel them to come in, so that my house may be filled.**

We certainly cannot compel them in some physical manner – i.e., by force. Our message and our manner of living must be such that there is reason beyond obligation to join us. The Bible tells us that we are living letters from God, "being known and being read by all men" (2 Corinthians 3:2).

Make it your goal to connect with as many people as possible to share the truth of God's Kingdom.

The Kingdom and the Church

Matthew 16:17-19
17 Jesus answered and said to him, "Blessed are you, Simon Bar-Jonah, for flesh and blood has not revealed this to you, but My Father who is in heaven.
18 And I also say to you that you are Peter, and on this rock I will build My church, and the gates of Hades shall not prevail against it.
19 And I will give you the keys of the kingdom of heaven, and whatever you bind on earth will be bound in heaven, and whatever you loose on earth will be loosed in heaven."

Acts 1:6 Therefore, when they had come together, they asked Him, saying, "Lord, will You at this time restore the kingdom to Israel?"

While there was slight confusion among the Twelve about what or who this Kingdom pertains, it is clear in the New Testament that the Church is the centerpiece of God's master plan. Revelation was progressive in Biblical times. As more came, it built upon the previous without canceling the latter. Here in Matthew 16, Jesus introduces the term "church" to the disciples. The Greek word is *ekklesia*, meaning "called out ones." The calling out comes from the revelation that Jesus is the Christ. This is the rock, or foundation upon which the church is built.

It is the *church* that the gates of hell cannot prevail against. Satan is always maneuvering to splinter off the believer from his or her covering – the church. This is because he can snipe the believer who is not sheltered within the safety of the church. I know that many people do not want to hear this. They choose to love the Bridegroom, Jesus, but reject the bride, the church. This cannot be. It is impermissible to God. *Husbands, love your wives, even as Christ also loved the church, and gave himself for it* (Ephesians 5:25). Christ loves the church and gave Himself for it.

The Kingdom is advanced through the church. The body of Christ is the conduit through which God advances His Kingdom. We are not talking about a piece of land or earthly titles. Conversion takes place in the hearts of people. There are several baptisms in Scripture (doctrine of baptisms, plural, Hebrews 6:2).

Four Main Baptisms

1. Baptism into Christ at conversion (Galatians 3:27).
2. Baptism into the Body, also at conversion (1 Corinthians 12:13).
3. Baptism in water, subsequent to conversion (Matthew 28:19).
4. Baptism with the Holy Spirit, also subsequent to conversion (Acts 1:5).

The first two happen at the same time and are what takes place at salvation. The third, water baptism, is an outward testimony of the inward work of grace. It points to both baptism into Christ and also baptism into His body. The fourth, the baptism with the Holy Spirit, is the empowerment for service. Please understand that one cannot be baptized into Christ without concurrently being baptized into the body of Christ – the church. We become one with Him, but also one with the church. To remain separate from the church is Kingdom revolt.

Jesus said that the church had the power to bind and loose and that heaven would correspond. This authority is given only to the church and is for the purpose of Kingdom advancement. Whenever anyone tries to breakup the unity of the church, God sees this as a serious issue. While there may be many religious organizations, there is only one church, with the local church being the indigenous expression.

One New Man

Right before Jesus ascended to heaven, the disciples asked Him, "Lord, will You at this time restore the kingdom to Israel?" Their focus was still on Israel. Yet Israel is *not* the centerpiece of God's plan for the ages. Their inheritance is a piece of land – real estate. That is not the Kingdom of God. God's plan was always "one new man," as stated in Ephesians.

Ephesians 2:15 Having abolished in His flesh the enmity, that is, the law of commandments

contained in ordinances, so as to create in Himself one new man from the two, thus making peace.

The one new man that Paul was referring to was made up of both Jews and Gentiles. The blood of Jesus removed the barrier between us (vv. 13-14). While God still has promises to fulfill to Israel, these will only be fulfilled as they become grafted back into the tree (Romans 11) that was planted in God's mind before the foundations of the world – the church!

There are some believers operating under the *Hebrew Roots Movement* that have an unbalanced focus. Their attention is on the *shadow* of the Old Covenant and not the *substance* of the New. While the Old Covenant feasts and holy days have significance that is historical, spiritual and even prophetic, it must not be forgotten that Jesus is our feast. He is the fulfillment. The Kingdom is advanced as we lift *Him* up, not the type and shadow.

On the other end of the spectrum, some have tried to completely do away with the significance of Israel. Going so far as to say that the church took the place of them and all of the future promises to them were transferred to the church. This is known as *replacement theology* – the church replaces Israel. This also is contrary to Scripture. At no point in either the Old or the New Testament is there any indication of this idea.

What God has done is tear down the middle wall of separation and make one new man – the church. Paul's writings (1 Corinthians 10:32) identify three groups of people in the earth:

1. Jews
2. Gentiles
3. The Church

Once a person in baptized into Christ and into His body, there is no more Jew or Gentile, but the church.

Kingdom living requires active church participation.

> **Hebrews 10:25 Not forsaking the assembling of ourselves together, as is the manner of some, but exhorting one another, and so much the more as you see the Day approaching.**

Generally speaking, visitors to your church are looking for reasons *not* to come back as soon as they walk in the door. They will find them. We must give them the one compelling reason to come back that overrides the negatives. No, it's not a great music program or awesome children's ministry. As important as those are, they can and will find flaws with them. The one compelling reason for them to come back is *life*. In the church, they find the life of God. When they come into contact with it, they may not be able explain it, but they cannot deny it.

When receiving the life of God into their hearts, the next step is to plug into the body and become an active member. When I say member, I'm not necessarily referring to a member of the *organization*, but rather a member of the living *organism* of the church – the body of Christ.

What should the local church look like? What if the Bible were the only source of information we had to build a church. In other words, no one in our group had ever had the experience of even attending a church service. All there was available to plan it and put it into practice was a Bible. I bet your looking for me to give you all the answers, nice and tidy with bullet points. Instead, I'm going to challenge you to get into the Word of God and ask the Holy Spirit to reveal His truth on the church.

Needs Theory vs. God's Kingdom

There was a famous psychologist named Abraham Maslow from the 20th century who published a paper in 1943 called "A Theory of Human Motivation." It became known as "Maslow's Hierarchy of Needs." His theory was based on the idea that lower level needs (also known as "deficit needs") have to be met first, in order to reach your full potential (self-actualization).

Below is a diagram depicting this theory.

Maslow's Theory of Need:

Being Needs

Self-actualization

Esteem

Belonging

Safety

Physiological

Deficit Needs

I first became acquainted with this theory while attending business leadership training conducted by retired military officers. I found the theory to be intriguing but lacking.

Maslow was correct in identifying the basic needs of humanity. But Jesus taught the opposite of this theory. He instructed us to seek God's Kingdom *first* and that all of our deficiency needs would be met

> **Matthew 6:33 But seek first the kingdom of God and His righteousness, and all these things shall be added to you.**

The *things* Jesus was speaking of are the very same ones that Maslow identified in his theory. Things such as safety and provision, love and belonging, esteem and purpose.

Those who are always in pursuit of the deficit needs will never find fulfillment.

> **Matthew 6:32 (NLT) These things dominate the thoughts of unbelievers, but your heavenly Father already knows all your needs.**

The reality is that if a person is not seeking the Kingdom of God first, there will always be a deficiency in the lower level needs. Let's examine these needs one at a time:

Physiological: Breathing, Food, Water, Sleep, Etc.

Safety: Physical Security, Employment, Health, Etc.

Belonging: Friendship, Family, Intimacy, Etc.

Esteem: Self-Esteem, Confidence, Achievement, Respect, Etc.

Self-actualization: Morality, Creativity, Spirituality, and Purpose (from a Christian perspective, this is where one would seek the Kingdom of God)

Self-Actualization occurs, Maslow theorized, when all of the lower level needs have been met. At this stage, the person finds their purpose for living, as well as the needed creativity and morality for fulfilling this purpose. This theory so conflicts with the Gospel message that it actually lands *opposite* of the Gospel.

If a person wants to find their purpose for living, the only way is to take up their cross and follow Jesus. The Kingdom is a paradox. If a person is focused on meeting their own needs, they will ultimately lose out on their purpose in life. But through putting God first and denying self, true self-actualization occurs – potential is reached.

Seek first the Kingdom of God and... God will meet your *physiological needs* of food, water and rest.

Seek first the Kingdom of God and... God will meet your *safety needs* of employment and health.

Seek first the Kingdom of God and... God will meet your *belonging needs* of a family and the right friends.

Seek first the Kingdom of God and… God will meet your *esteem needs* of achievement and respect.

Keep in mind that God will meet your *needs*, not your *greeds*. The Bible warns us that in the last days people will be lovers of self.

> **2 Timothy 3:1-2**
> **1 But know this, that in the last days perilous times will come:**
> **2 For men will be lovers of themselves…**

That prophecy is certainly being fulfilled before our very eyes. Today is perhaps the most narcissistic society in the history of civilization. Narcissus was a mythical Greek god who fell in love with his own reflection. He could never love a woman because none compared with his own beauty.

The Kingdom of God is a paradox; in other words, there are many *apparent* contradictions. For example, if you seek to preserve your life you lose it and if you seek to lose your life you save it (Luke 17:33).

The idea that if you meet lower level needs that it will ultimately meet with fulfillment is a trap of Satan. In fact, Jesus said that you could gain the whole world and lose your own soul in the process (Mark 8:36).

Let's examine a short parable of Jesus, in relation to this concept.

Matthew 13:45-46
45 "Again, the kingdom of heaven is like a merchant seeking beautiful pearls,
46 who, when he had found one pearl of great price, went and sold all that he had and bought it.

The King, Jesus, is the Pearl of great price. When a person finds Him, it happens with a realization that nothing else in life – no other need – compares with the beauty of this precious Pearl. The focus goes off of *deficit needs* and onto Jesus. This doesn't happen due to some kind of religious reform or self-help effort. Jesus heals the brokenness in the soul that was caused by sin. Pursuit of worldly things and relationships cannot fix that problem. Reaching fulfillment can only truly be accomplished through finding Jesus.

The rich young ruler in Matthew 19:16-22 was found to be in conflict between his desire to please God and his love for worldly treasure. Jesus told him to sell all that he had and give it to the poor and to come follow Him. This saddened the man because he had lots of possessions. Better stated, the possessions had him. Instead of following Jesus, the man sorrowfully walked away. Why would Jesus ask this man to sell everything and give it to the poor as a prerequisite to following Him? He didn't require this of others. Jesus knew that this rich young ruler's heart was entangled with the love of money. In order for him to be free, it was going to take a radical change. The man mistakenly thought that by giving up his wealth, he would incur too many needs. The reality is that all of his needs would have been met by following Jesus.

The Word of the Kingdom

The Parable of the Sower

In Matthew 13:18-23, Jesus talked about four kinds of hearts related to the "word of the Kingdom." Which kind are you?

> **18 "Therefore hear the parable of the sower:**
> **19 When anyone hears the word of the kingdom, and does not understand it, then the wicked one comes and snatches away what was sown in his heart. This is he who received seed by the wayside.**
> **20 But he who received the seed on stony places, this is he who hears the word and immediately receives it with joy;**
> **21 yet he has no root in himself, but endures only for a while. For when tribulation or persecution arises because of the word, immediately he stumbles.**
> **22 Now he who received seed among the thorns is he who hears the word, and the cares of this world and the deceitfulness of riches choke the word, and he becomes unfruitful.**
> **23 But he who received seed on the good ground is he who hears the word and understands it, who indeed bears fruit and**

produces: some a hundredfold, some sixty, some thirty."

1. The Wayside Heart:

   When anyone hears the word of the kingdom, and does not understand it, then the wicked one comes and snatches away what was sown in his heart. This is he who received seed by the wayside.

When He hears the Word of God, he allows the devil to snatch the Word out of his heart. The word "snatch" in the Greek means, "to seize upon openly with force." These are those who mentally agree with the Word, and may even emotionally respond, but don't allow the Word to get into their hearts. Satan is able to attack them quickly with temptation and pull them away.

The Bible refers to Satan as the one who blinds the minds of unbelievers.

> **2 Corinthians 4: 3-4**
> **3 But even if our gospel is veiled, it is veiled to those who are perishing,**
> **4 whose minds the god of this age has blinded, who do not believe, lest the light of the gospel of the glory of Christ, who is the image of God, should shine on them**

In your intercessory prayer time, come against the spiritual blindness that is over the area where you live.

2. The Stony Heart:

But he who received the seed on stony places, this is he who hears the word and immediately receives it with joy; yet he has no root in himself, but endures only for a while. For when tribulation or persecution arises because of the word, immediately he stumbles.

When he hears the Word of God, he immediately responds outwardly. This person gets all excited about what he has heard, but doesn't allow the Word to take root. As a consequence, he only endures for a while. He is not prepared for the persecution that will arise for the Word's sake. Make no mistake... when you openly declare God's Word, be prepared to be attacked. Notice that he "immediately" receives the Word, and "immediately" falls away.

If there is one thing that Satan fears it is a child of God who gets rooted and grounded in the Word of God. This is why he attacks early and often whenever you decide to make a commitment to the Word. Getting rooted is critical to being built up. Without the root system a tree cannot stand. The roots of a tree spread twice as wide as the circumference of the tree's branches.

Colossians 2:7 rooted and built up in Him and established in the faith, as you have been taught.

3. The Thorny Heart:

Now he who received seed among the thorns is he who hears the word, and the cares of this world and the deceitfulness of riches choke the word, and he becomes unfruitful.

This person hears the Word of God, but does not allow it to deal with his heart to root out the thorns that are already present. He appears to be making progress. But when life's pressures come, the thorns that are already there begin to manifest. The cares of this world choke out the Word of God. A person cannot serve both God and mammon.

There comes a point in every believer's walk with God where you have to count the cost, take up your cross and follow Him. Jesus clearly taught that the way to eternal life was narrow and difficult. You cannot take along all of the baggage of the world. The cares of this life and the pursuit of material things will eventually choke out the Word of God.

Hebrews 12:1-2
1 Therefore we also, since we are surrounded by so great a cloud of witnesses, let us lay aside every weight, and the sin which so easily ensnares us, and let us run with endurance the race that is set before us,
2 looking unto Jesus, the author and finisher of our faith, who for the joy that was set before Him

endured the cross, despising the shame, and has sat down at the right hand of the throne of God.

It is not only the sins that will keep us defeated but the extra weight that we try to carry. Eventually, they will choke out the Word of God and bring defeat.

4. **The Good Ground Heart:**

But he who received seed on the good ground is he who hears the word and understands it, who indeed bears fruit and produces: some a hundredfold, some sixty, some thirty.

This person hears the Word of God and receives it; he applies it to understanding, allowing the Word to change the inward man. He allows it to renew his mind to begin a new pattern of thinking. The Greek word for "receive" means, "to embrace with assent and obedience." It is not enough to hear and receive the Word of God; one must obey the Word. This person is known by the fruit, which he bears.

James 1:22 says, "But be doers of the word, and not hearers only, deceiving yourselves." When we act on the Word, change and fruit are produced in our lives. Weakness leaves and strength rises up. Our vocabulary changes – we no longer go around talking defeat, but boldness is in our voice as we declare that we can do all things through Christ Jesus Who strengthens us. Instead of needing ministered to all of the time, we now become the one who ministers to others. This person feeds on the meat of God's Word and walks in the Spirit.

This person is a Kingdom advancer.

Isn't it time to become that person?

Sadly, Jesus said that only 25% of those who hear the Word of God are actually going to produce fruit in their lives. The choice is up to us. Choose to be a Good Ground Heart.

The Provision of the Kingdom

There are more than 2,000 references in the Bible on the topic of finances and/or material possessions. Kingdom living requires stewardship. Obviously, this is an important topic to God. Generally speaking, there has been a real lack of balance in teaching on this subject. There are extremes on both sides – those who focus too much on giving and finances and those who say too little.

But if we are going to advance the Kingdom of God in this temporary realm, it will require the currency of this dispensation. Unfortunately, money controls a lot of people's hearts and becomes a stumbling block in their service to God.

Seek First the Kingdom of God

As we previously discussed, the Kingdom operates contrary to the theory of needs that modern psychology sets forth.

> **Matthew 6:33 But seek first the kingdom of God and His righteousness, and all these things shall be added to you.**

Once more, we find Jesus discussing the Kingdom of God. Here, in the Sermon on the Mount, Jesus speaks on the matter of *priorities*. He clearly sets forth the singular priority of a Kingdom citizen: seek first the Kingdom of God.

127

> **Matthew 6:31-32**
> **31 "Therefore do not worry, saying, 'What shall we eat?' or 'What shall we drink?' or 'What shall we wear?'**
> **32 For after all these things the Gentiles seek. For your heavenly Father knows that you need all these things.**

The Gentiles represented all of those who were *outside* of the covenant of God. Covenant, basically means that everything your covenant partner has belongs to you and everything you have belongs to your covenant partner. The Father knows what our needs are before we ask, and has made provision to meet those needs. Our calling is to seek Him, not for what He gives us, but for who He is.

Notice that Jesus did not say to seek all these other things second. He said that all we have need of would be *added* to us – the added blessing of God. Many Christians have fallen into the unfortunate habit of chasing God's blessing. However, Scripture is clear that when we are aligned with God's will for our lives, the blessing will follow us.

> **Deuteronomy 28:2 And all these blessings shall come upon you and overtake you, because you obey the voice of the Lord your God.**

To refresh, here are the key words of this powerful statement made by Jesus in Matthew 6:33:

1. Seek (the desire of our heart)
2. First (the priority of our life)
3. Kingdom of God (our citizenship)
4. Righteousness (Kingdom conduct)
5. Things (material goods and finances)
6. Added (God's provision)

The Law of Reciprocity

The Law of Reciprocity is a Kingdom principle. The word reciprocity means mutuality. This key is highlighted in Jesus' statement recorded in Luke 6:38.

> **Luke 6:38 Give, and it will be given to you: good measure, pressed down, shaken together, and running over will be put into your bosom. For with the same measure that you use, it will be measured back to you.**

The verb "give" is in the present, continuous tense, while the verb for "it will be given" is in the future tense. When we give, we are procuring God's blessing on our future. Many times, Christians will postpone giving until a more advantageous time occurs. This limits the hand of God in the area of financial blessing. The Bible tells us that if we *cast our bread upon the waters, we will find it after many days* (Ecclesiastes 11:1). When we give into the Kingdom of God, it leaves our hand, but never leaves our life.

Jesus said that the same measure that we use would be measured back to us again. Or in other words, as the New Living Translation renders this: "The amount you give will determine the amount you get back." This is not to say that we are to give for the purpose of getting back. That is not the intent of the message. The Christian walk is one governed by motive and attitude. We are to give in order to advance the Kingdom.

The Philippians learned this valuable lesson through their giving to the Apostle Paul's ministry.

> **Philippians 4:15-19**
> **15 Now you Philippians know also that in the beginning of the gospel, when I departed from Macedonia, no church shared with me concerning giving and receiving but you only.**
> **16 For even in Thessalonica you sent aid once and again for my necessities.**
> **17 Not that I seek the gift, but I seek the fruit that abounds to your account.**
> **18 Indeed I have all and abound. I am full, having received from Epaphroditus the things sent from you, a sweet-smelling aroma, an acceptable sacrifice, well pleasing to God.**
> **19 And my God shall supply all your need according to His riches in glory by Christ Jesus.**

Your Treasure & Your Heart

As much as the Bible has to say about material possessions, it is important to remember that Jesus said, "Where your treasure is, there will your heart be also" (Luke 12:34).

Matthew 6:24 No one can serve two masters; for either he will hate the one and love the other, or else he will be loyal to the one and despise the other. You cannot serve God and mammon.

Provision comes from whole-hearted commitment and willingness to surrender all to Him. The merchant who found the pearl of great price in Matthew 13:45-46 was willing to liquidate all his assets to buy the one pearl, which represented Jesus and the Kingdom. The disciples were willing to forsake their fishing nets to follow Jesus.

Tithing

Let's talk about the concept of tithing for a moment. Tithing originated in the Old Testament. Does that mean that it has no relevance to the New Testament follower of Christ? Some would say that it was under the Law, therefore, has no application under grace. However, tithing began way before the Law, at least as early as Abraham. Hebrews 7:2 says that Abraham gave a tenth part of all. He actually referred to tithing as "lifting my hand to the Yahweh" (Genesis 14:22).

Under the New Covenant, tithing is not required in a legalistic manner. God wants a cheerful giver, not one who gives out of obligation. But when a person understands the blessing that is associated with the tithe, and what it truly means to put God first in the area of finances, it can totally change their life.

First off, tithing does not mean that 90% belongs to you and 10% belongs to God. The tithe, given off the top, means that everything belongs to God and you are giving Him the first 10% to demonstrate this with more than words. That now places the giver into the role of steward. And God is able to do more with 90% than you can do with 100%.

Listen to these great words in the book of Malachi:

> **Malachi 3:10 Bring all the tithes into the storehouse, that there may be food in My house, and try [prove] Me now in this," says the Lord of hosts, "If I will not open for you the windows of heaven and pour out for you such blessing that there will not be room enough to receive it.**

Further, in the next verse, God said that He would rebuke the devourer for your sakes. Satan wants to keep you in financial bondage because he understands that the borrower is servant to the lender (Proverbs 22:7). But God wants to break the spirit of poverty off your life. The spirit of poverty is the fear that you don't have enough to give to God and have enough left over to live on.

In Malachi 3:10, God said to "Prove Me." In other words, put Him to the test. This word means "to examine," which is different than provoking Him with doubt and rebellion. God is challenging His people to investigate His goodness and see how very much He desires to bless them.

Kingdom Attitudes

Kingdom attitudes are revealed in the Sermon on the Mount, in the Beatitudes.

> **Matthew 5:3-10**
> **3 "Blessed are the poor in spirit, for theirs is the kingdom of heaven.**
> **4 Blessed are those who mourn, for they shall be comforted.**
> **5 Blessed are the meek, for they shall inherit the earth.**
> **6 Blessed are those who hunger and thirst for righteousness, for they shall be filled.**
> **7 Blessed are the merciful, for they shall obtain mercy.**
> **8 Blessed are the pure in heart, for they shall see God.**
> **9 Blessed are the peacemakers, for they shall be called sons of God.**
> **10 Blessed are those who are persecuted for righteousness' sake, for theirs is the kingdom of heaven.**

The word "beatitude" comes from the Latin *beatitudo*, meaning "blessedness." The phrase "blessed are" in each of the beatitudes implies a current state of happiness or well-being. While speaking of a current "blessedness," each pronouncement also promises a future reward.

These are inward qualities, produced by the Holy Spirit, through relationship with Jesus. Most seek for happiness or blessedness through external activity, but true blessing comes from within a person.

We will look at each of the beatitudes, their meaning and the blessing associated with them.

Beatitude 1: Poor in Spirit

Meaning

> To be poor in spirit is the acknowledgment that we are not self-sufficient. The Greek word for "poor" is *ptochos* (pto-khos) and means, "destitute of wealth, influence, position, honor."

> When one gets to the end of himself, he gets to the beginning of God.

Blessing

> Theirs is the kingdom of heaven.

> Romans 14:17 says, "The kingdom of God is ... righteousness and peace and joy in the Holy Spirit."

> Kingdom possession belongs to all who are poor in spirit and whose trust is in the Lord.

Beatitude 2: Those who mourn

Meaning

The closer one gets to God, the more personal sin causes mourning in the heart of the child of God. The Greek word for "mourn" is *pentheo* (pen-theh-o) and means, "the feeling and act of sorrow and grief."

Blessing

They shall be comforted.

The comfort of the Holy Spirit is upon the life of all with a repentant heart. The Greek word for "comfort" is *parakaleo* (par-ak-al-eh-o) and means, "called alongside to help."

Beatitude 3: Meek

Meaning

Meekness is *not* weakness! In fact, the Greek word for "meek" is *praus* (prah-ooce) and was used to describe warhorses. A "meek" horse was one under the control of its master, even though it had tremendous power and ability.

Meekness toward God is that disposition of spirit that accepts His dealings with us as good and therefore without disputing or resisting.

Blessing

They shall inherit the earth.

The meek in God will rule together with Christ because they can be trusted and are under His control.

Beatitude 4: Hunger and Thirst for Righteousness

Meaning

The appetite of the follower of Christ has been radically been changed. He no longer desires the things of the world, but more of Him.

The Greek word for "hunger" is *peinao* (pi-nah-o) and means, "to crave ardently, to seek with eager desire."

The Greek word for "thirst" is *dipsao* (dip-sah-o) and means, "to painfully feel the want of and eagerly want for."

If you want to be blessed, have a passion for Jesus!

Blessing

They shall be filled.

Basically, we each have as much of God as we want. If we want more of Him, we will hunger and thirst for Him. Jeremiah 29:13 says, "And you will seek Me and find Me, when you search for Me with all your heart."

Beatitude 5: Merciful

Meaning

The merciful are blessed because they have learned one of life's great secrets. Forgive and show mercy.

"Merciful" in the Greek is *eleeo* (el-eh-eh-o) and means, "to have compassion, to show mercy, to help the afflicted."

Blessing

They shall obtain mercy.

Give and it shall be given unto you. The law of sowing and reaping are no truer than in the area of mercy. If you desire God's mercy and the mercy of others, then you must be one who shows mercy.

Beatitude 6: Pure in Heart

Meaning

There is a difference between purity and holiness. To be holy means to be free from contamination; to be pure means to be free from mixture.

The Greek word for "pure" is *katharos* (kath-ar-os) and is a powerful word. It has the following meanings:

- Cleansed like a vine by pruning (John. 15)
- Free from corrupt desire, from sin and guilt
- Free from every mixture of what is false
- Blameless, innocent

Blessing

They shall see God.

Isn't this one obvious? We cannot see God when we have a divided heart. He demands our undivided attention from a pure heart that is free from the mixture of this world.

Beatitude 7: Peacemakers

Meaning

There is a great difference between a "peacekeeper" and a "peacemaker." The former never rocks the boat and rarely deals with the root cause of the issue, choosing rather to appease the personalities involved. The latter, however, will confront and challenge in order to make peace.

The Greek word for "peace" is *eirene* (i-ray-nay) and means, "peace between individuals, i.e., harmony, concord."

Blessing

They shall be called sons of God.

"Sons" is from the Greek word *huios* (hwee-os) and means "position of privilege." This is the same word used in Romans 8:14, "For as many as are led by the Spirit of God are the sons of God."

Peacemaking is an endeavor that must be initiated and led by the Holy Spirit. It should not be an undertaking of the flesh.

Beatitude 8: Persecuted for Righteousness' Sake

Meaning

In the United States we don't fully appreciate what it means to be persecuted for Christ. Consider the following:

- It is estimated that currently over 200 million Christians are being persecuted worldwide.
- More Christians were martyred in the 20th century than in all previous centuries combined.

- An average of 159,960 Christians worldwide are martyred for their faith per year.
- Persecution, however, is on the rise in the U.S. It manifest in different forms. Being a bold witness for Jesus will always meet with resistance from the world. They hate us because they first hated Jesus.

Blessing

Theirs is the kingdom of heaven.

We have an ever-present reminder that our citizenship is in heaven (Philippians 3:20). We are just passing through.

The early disciples gladly gave their lives for the cause of Christ. All of the original apostles were martyred except John.

There is a crown of life awaiting those who are persecuted (Rev. 2:10).

The Temporal Aspects of the Kingdom

> **Hebrews 2:8 You have put all things in subjection under his feet." For in that He put all in subjection under him, He left nothing that is not put under him. But now we do not yet see all things put under him.**

Through the finished work of the Cross, Satan has been eternally defeated. All things are *under* the feet of Jesus. However, in this temporary dispensation, the earth is still under the curse of sin.

"But now…"

We know that many things are God's perfect will, but they do not *automatically* happen. If so, Jesus would not have taught us to pray, "Your kingdom come. Your will be done, on earth as it is in heaven." There is a vast difference between heaven, which speaks of the eternal and that which is perfect, and earth, with speaks of the temporal and imperfection. The latter is the *now* of "but now."

When Jesus was on the earth, He healed all who were oppressed of the devil (Acts 10:38). This revealed the will of the Father. Multiple times in the Gospels it is indicated that Jesus "healed them all." However, today we do not see everyone being healed. Has

God's will changed? Certainly not. There are many variables related to why someone may not be healed. Consider the following, which is not meant to be exhaustive:

- **Timing:** There are occasions when the afflicted must keep standing for healing. When the lame man was healed in Acts 3, thousands came to Christ. God may be timing a healing in order to reach the most people for the Kingdom.

- **Demonic opposition:** In Mark 9, the disciples could not deliver the deaf and mute boy and Jesus told them that because of the demonic involvement, additional prayer and fasting was necessary.

- **Lack of faith:** On 12 different occasions Jesus told someone who was healed, "According to your faith be it unto you."

- **Unforgiveness:** Perhaps nothing quenches God's healing flow more than unforgiveness (Mark 11:25).

- **Poor diet:** If we are putting contamination into our bodies and abusing it with poor diet, we are working *against* the healing power of God.

- **Sinful lifestyle:** When King Hezekiah repented, God added 15 years to his life (Isaiah 38:5).

There are many other reasons that healing may be delayed or not received at all. Too often, folks jump immediately on the *lack of faith* reason. But this is not always the case. In fact, there have been numerous *word of faith* teachers who have died from illness and disease in recent years. Their doctrine contended that sickness always came from unbelief and that healing would always come if there were faith. However, their personal results didn't measure up to their teaching.

We are living in a sin-cursed world and Satan has been allowed to continue in this probationary stage of humanity in order to test the free will of man. God wants worshippers, not robots. We don't *see* all things under Jesus' feet in this moment, but there is coming a day of full redemption for humanity and all creation. This is exactly what Paul described in his letter to the Romans.

> **Romans 8:18-25**
> **18 For I consider that the sufferings of this present time are not worthy to be compared with the glory which shall be revealed in us.**
> **19 For the earnest expectation of the creation eagerly waits for the revealing of the sons of God.**
> **20 For the creation was subjected to futility, not willingly, but because of Him who subjected it in hope;**
> **21 because the creation itself also will be delivered from the bondage of corruption into the glorious liberty of the children of God.**

22 For we know that the whole creation groans and labors with birth pangs together until now.

23 Not only that, but we also who have the firstfruits of the Spirit, even we ourselves groan within ourselves, eagerly waiting for the adoption, the redemption of our body.

24 For we were saved in this hope, but hope that is seen is not hope; for why does one still hope for what he sees?

25 But if we hope for what we do not see, we eagerly wait for it with perseverance.

Notice that Paul compared and contrasted "present time" with future "glory" (v 18). This was further analogized by comparing the corruption of our present bodies with the glorious liberty that will transpire when our bodies will be redeemed through the resurrection. Because we have this hope as believers, we both eagerly wait and persevere. To wait assumes a delay, but to be eager conveys a zeal and fervor.

John the revelator spoke of that day when every tear would be wiped away.

> **Revelation 21:4** And God will wipe away every tear from their eyes; there shall be no more death, nor sorrow, nor crying. There shall be no more pain, for the former things have passed away."

Consider the differences between the temporary and the eternal aspects of God's Kingdom:

Temporary	Eternal
• Death • Sorrow • Pain • Opposition • Tribulation • Temptation	• No more more death • No more Sorrow • No more pain • No opposition – Satan bound • No more tribulation • Temptation ended

When Adam and Eve sinned in the garden, the earth, along with mankind, was placed under the curse of sin. This is a fallen world that has not yet been redeemed. The only thing that has been redeemed in this fallen world is the soul of every person who becomes born again. The sin-cursed earth will not be redeemed until Jesus sets up His physical Kingdom. Until such time, there is a conflict. This conflict comes in the form of death, sorrow, pain, opposition, temptation and tribulation.

But we were built for eternity. The *earth suit* (i.e., the physical body) that we now possess will go back to the dust of the ground. It will not be needed in the eternal Kingdom of God. Paul told the Corinthians, "For we know that if the earthly tent we live in is destroyed, we have a building from God, an eternal house in heaven, not built by human hands" (2 Corinthians 5:1). He went on to say, "Meanwhile we groan,

146

longing to be clothed instead with our heavenly dwelling" (v 2). This life on earth is the *meanwhile*. Our spirits groan within to be suited up with the heavenly and eternal suit. The groan is due to the conflict.

The one thing that is certain is that we will not understand everything that transpires in this physical life. The Bible declares, "We see through a glass darkly" (1 Corinthians 13:12 KJV). The Darby translation says, "For we see now through a dim window obscurely." The measure of faith that God has given each of us (Romans 12:3) is sufficient to help us navigate this rocky landscape.

The King is Coming Back!

Revelation 3:11 Behold, I am coming quickly! Hold fast what you have, that no one may take your crown.

While the Kingdom of God is assuredly *within* us, there is also a literal fulfillment of the eternal Kingdom of God. The aspect of the Kingdom that our hearts long for is the final redemption of all creation – from our corruptible bodies to the earth itself.

> **Romans 8:18-25**
> **18 For I consider that the sufferings of this present time are not worthy to be compared with the glory which shall be revealed in us.**
> **19 For the earnest expectation of the creation eagerly waits for the revealing of the sons of God.**
> **20 For the creation was subjected to futility, not willingly, but because of Him who subjected it in hope;**
> **21 because the creation itself also will be delivered from the bondage of corruption into the glorious liberty of the children of God.**
> **22 For we know that the whole creation groans and labors with birth pangs together until now.**

23 Not only that, but we also who have the firstfruits of the Spirit, even we ourselves groan within ourselves, eagerly waiting for the adoption, the redemption of our body.
24 For we were saved in this hope, but hope that is seen is not hope; for why does one still hope for what he sees?
25 But if we hope for what we do not see, we eagerly wait for it with perseverance.

That day is unquestionably coming. It is the blessed hope of every true believer. While the Bible does not completely connect the dots on the order of events, there are definite markers laid out. For example, a student of the Word cannot go to a single passage or verse and prove the timing of the rapture. However, we are told to rightly divide the Word (2 Timothy 2:15). This means we should review the entirety of the Word and allow Scripture to interpret Scripture.

There are four main views, with many subsets of belief that fall under each one.

1. Dispensational Premillennialism
2. Historical Premillennialism
3. Amillennialism
4. Postmillennialism

As you may guess, the Millennial Reign of Christ is the centerpiece for each view.

Dispensational Premillennialism	
Does Jesus Return?	Yes

When Does Jesus Return?	After the 7-year tribulation period
When is the Rapture?	Before the 7-year tribulation period
Is there a Literal 7-Year Great Tribulation?	Yes
Is the Millennium Literal?	Yes there is a literal 1,000 year reign
Does Israel have a role in Future Events?	Yes, God will restore the nation of Israel (they will turn to Jesus) and graft them into the church in the kingdom

Historical Premillennialism	
Does Jesus Return?	Yes
When Does Jesus Return?	After the 7-year tribulation period
When is the Rapture?	After the 7-year tribulation period
Is there a Literal 7-Year Great Tribulation?	Yes
Is the Millennium Literal?	Yes there is a literal 1,000 year reign
Does Israel have a role in Future Events?	No, only spiritual "Israel" (the church) has any role in the future kingdom

Amillennialism	
Does Jesus Return?	Yes
When Does Jesus	Anytime. All prophetic

Return?	timetables are spiritual not literal
When is the Rapture?	After the Millennium, which is spiritual and ongoing
Is there a Literal 7-Year Great Tribulation?	No, this refers to general tribulation and persecution throughout the history of the church
Is the Millennium Literal?	No, this refers only to a spiritual kingdom
Does Israel have a role in Future Events?	No, only spiritual "Israel" (the church) has any role in the future kingdom

Postmillennialism	
Does Jesus Return?	Yes
When Does Jesus Return?	After the spiritual "millennium" (the church will become prosperous and dominant and usher back Jesus)
When is the Rapture?	After
Is there a Literal 7-Year Great Tribulation?	No, this refers to the first century Jewish-Roman war
Is the Millennium Literal?	No, this refers to a golden age for the church where the church, in essence, sets up the "kingdom" and is dominant in the earth.
Does Israel have a	No, only spiritual "Israel" (the

role in Future Events?	church) has any role in the future kingdom

All premillennial believers agree on the following things:

- There will be a rapture (disagreement on the timing).
- There is a literal Millennial Reign of Christ.
- Jesus will physically return before the Millennium and will reign one thousand years prior to the eternal kingdom of God.

Shown below are graphical representations of the three primary premillennial views.

Pre-Tribulation View

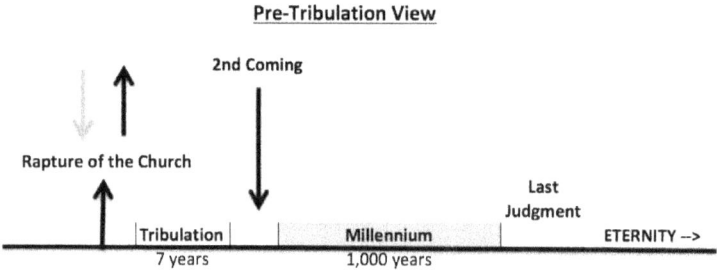

2nd Coming

Rapture of the Church

Last Judgment

Tribulation | Millennium | ETERNITY -->
7 years | 1,000 years

Mid-Tribulation View

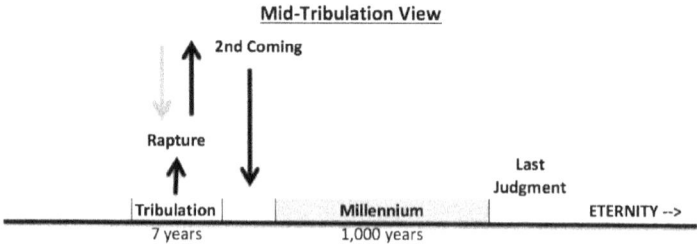

2nd Coming

Rapture

Last Judgment

Tribulation | Millennium | ETERNITY -->
7 years | 1,000 years

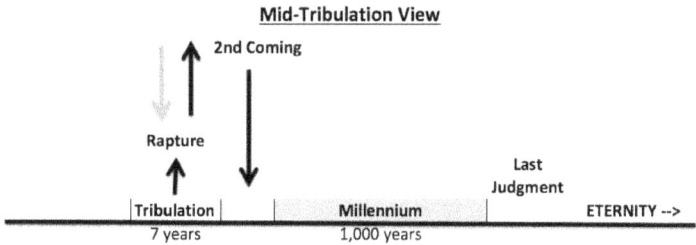

Mid-Tribulation View

The following is my interpretation from Scripture on the order of end-time events surrounding the Second Coming and eternal Kingdom:

1. **The rapture of the church** (1 Thessalonians 4:13-18). I believe this to be the first event related to the Second Coming of Christ. This is not the Second Coming, as Christ only returns to the clouds and not the earth at the rapture. In fulfillment of Jesus' words, the pre-tribulation rapture of the church is the only timing that satisfies Matthew 24:36: "But concerning that day and hour no one knows."

2. **Believers appear before the judgment seat of Christ** to receive rewards (2 Corinthians 5:10). This occurs immediately following the rapture. It is not a judgment to determine one's eternal destiny, but to issue rewards. This is the occasion when we will give an account of what we did with the will of God for our lives. Did we live out our God-given destiny and use our gifts for His glory?

3. **The first seal is loosed**: the antichrist is revealed (Revelation 6:2). The Holy Spirit empowered

church is the restraining force that is holding back the man of sin from being revealed (2 Thessalonians 2:8). When the church is taken out – just as Lot was taken out Sodom and as Noah entered the Ark, evil will ensue.

4. **The seven-year tribulation period** on earth (Matthew 24:21). We know that this period of time is seven years because of the prophecy in the book of Daniel regarding the 70 weeks of years. There remains one week of years (7 years) to be fulfilled. Further, this week of years was related to Daniel's people (Israel), not the church (Daniel 9:24). Jeremiah refers to the period as, "The time of Jacob's trouble" (Jeremiah 30:7). Jacob always refers to Israel in Scripture, without exception. These are the saints spoken of in Revelation after the first three chapters. These seven years are ordained to usher Israel back into God's program and save them in order that they may enter God's eternal kingdom.

5. **The Second Coming**: Jesus comes back with the army of saints (Revelation 19:11-16). The Bible says that the church – His bride clothed in fine linen, will be following Jesus on white horses. If the church was on the earth during the tribulation this would not be possible. Jude 14 also says that the Lord will be coming with ten thousands (i.e., innumerable) of His saints. When Jesus comes the second time, He will return as conquering King, not as the suffering servant as He did in His first coming.

6. **Armageddon**: the armies of the Antichrist are defeated (Revelation 19:19-21). All of the Antichrist's armies and their collective force will gather in the valley of Armageddon for the final showdown. It will not be much of a battle, as Christ will destroy them with the brightness of His coming.

    2 Thessalonians 2:8 And then the lawless one will be revealed, whom the Lord will consume with the breath of His mouth and destroy with the brightness of His coming.

7. **Satan is cast into the bottomless pit** for 1,000 years (Revelation 20:1-3). This is the length of Christ's Millennial Reign. The full and complete doom of Satan is on hold during this period while he is bound up in the bottomless pit. His final punishment will occur at the conclusion of the 1,000 years.

8. **Jesus sets up His Millennial Kingdom** (Revelation 20:6). There are some who do not believe in a literal one-thousand-year reign of Christ, but the Bible uses the phrase "the thousand years" six times in the passage of Revelation 20:2-7. Jesus will rule as King over Israel and the nations and the church will rule and reign with Him. As mentioned in point 7, Satan will be bound during this period. The earth will be in complete peace (Isaiah 11:6-9).

9. **Those left on earth that did not take the mark of the beast will be allowed to enter the kingdom in their natural bodies.** The natural people who weren't resurrected will produce children during the millennial kingdom (Zechariah 14:16; Isaiah 65:20-23). This fact is often unknown by Christians, or spiritualized by some who do not take Bible prophecy literally.

10. **At the end of the 1,000 years**, Satan will be loosed for a short season and gather up the natural people who want to rebel. Fire will come down from heaven and destroy them and Satan will be cast into the Lake of Fire for eternity (Revelation 20:7-10).

11. **The Great White Throne (GWT) judgment** will occur for all of the unsaved and they will be transferred from Hades to the Lake of Fire for eternity (Revelation 20:11-15). Both the temporary abode of Hades and the eternal abode of the Lake of Fire are literal places of torment. The GWT judgment is not for believers – those who are saved. This is the final judgment of the unsaved.

12. **God will renovate the earth into a state of eternal perfection** (2 Peter 3:10; Revelation 21). The earth has been under the curse of sin for over 6,000 years – since the fall of Adam in the garden. At this time, the redemption of the earth, and all creation will take place. The earth will not be destroyed, but instead renovated by glorious fire. God's very

specific reason for doing this is revealed in the last point below.

13. **The heavenly city New Jerusalem comes down** from God the Father, out of heaven to the earth and the Father establishes His throne on the new earth and dwells with His people forever (Revelation 21:2-3). New Jerusalem has the very specific dimensions of 1,500 miles wide, 1,500 miles deep, and 1,500 miles high (Revelation 21:15-16).

    The height of the city is very interesting. If there are skyscrapers in the city, they can reach more than 600,000 floors. There will be enough room in New Jerusalem for every person that has been born from Adam and Eve all the way to the last baby born in the future – plus billions more! This really drives home the Lord's heart, that He is not willing that any should perish but that all should come to repentance (2 Peter 3:9).

Advancing the Kingdom

Matthew 24:14 And this gospel of the kingdom will be preached in all the world as a witness to all the nations, and then the end will come.

Our mission is to advance the Kingdom. To advance means to "expand and spread." So many people look at the condition of society and see the evil that is progressively worsening and lose hope. However, the Bible clearly warns us of such times at the end of the age. Paul wrote to Timothy that "evil men and seducers will go from bad to worse" (2 Timothy 3:13) and that "some would abandon the faith and following deceiving spirits" (1 Timothy 4:1).

None of this evil activity will be able to prevent the church from advancing the Kingdom. As the darkness gets darker, the Lord's glory will increase upon His people (Isaiah 60:1). There is a dividing line between the true church and the apostate church that is becoming clearer by the day.

Let's take a moment and examine the literalness of Jesus' statement in Matthew 24. The Greek word for "nations" is *ethnos*, from which we derive the word *ethnic*. It is referring to *people groups*, not political states. There are close to 17,000 people groups in the world. We are approaching the fulfillment of this prophecy. However, there remains close to 3,000 people groups where there is no viable Christian testimony. This does not mean that the Gospel has not been preached there, but that there is no fruit in terms of a Christian presence. Clearly, there remains work to be done.

Luke 19:13 Occupy till I come

What does it mean to occupy? Literally, the original word means to "do business." What is the business of the church? To advance the Kingdom. The church is not in the business of entertaining. Our job is not to erect buildings or even build large crowds. There is a difference between building a church and building a crowd. The latter advances the Kingdom.

Time is so very short. It's crucial that we focus on the God-sized task in front of us and not get caught up in petty and inconsequential affairs. The Bible doesn't give formulas on how to advance the Kingdom, but there are some definite principles that are set forth in the New Testament. If we simply narrow things down to the Great Commission and the Great Commandment, we will be on the right track.

The Great Commandment

1. **Worship**: "Love the Lord your God with all your heart…" (Mark 12:30)

2. **Ministry/Service**: "Love your neighbor as yourself" (Mark 12:31)

The Great Commission

3. **Evangelism**: "Go into all the world and preach the gospel to every creature" (Mark 16:15)

4. **Build the Church**: "Baptizing them…" (Matthew 28:19)

5. **Make Disciples**: "Make disciples… teaching them to observe all things I have commanded you" (Matthew 28:19-20)

In advancing the Kingdom, the business of the church is not to *make* the Gospel relevant to modern society. Rather, it is to *show* the relevance of the Gospel. The Gospel was built for the ages; no additives needed; no extractions permitted. On the other hand, we should not be duped into thinking that 1950's Christianity is the Biblical model. "The good old days" as it is said. God is not stuck in a time warp. He is never changing yet always fresh.

There is the matter of contextualization. This is the ability of making the Gospel authentically experienced in each and every human situation. A study of the book of Acts shows that Paul deliberately addressed his Jewish listeners differently than he addressed pagan philosophers. Yet he had the same goal – to win them to Christ.

Paul stated his ministry philosophy clearly to the Corinthians:

> **1 Corinthians 9:22 I have become all things to all men, that I might by all means save some.**

Yet, for sure, Paul never compromised the Gospel. Advancing the Kingdom is not about promoting our traditions and preferences. Jesus said that it was possible to make the Word of God ineffective or useless through the tradition of men (Mark 7:13). The only thing that will have lasting effect and produce true Kingdom advancement is the power of the Gospel – God's Word.

The Bible calls believers *living epistles*, known and read by everyone (2 Corinthians 3:2). This means that the Word of the Kingdom becomes incarnated or personified in us. It isn't that we are just telling people words from off the pages of a book. The letter does not advance the Kingdom, but the Spirit. The Spirit lives inside of His people – the Kingdom of God is within us.

The root Hebrew word for "testimony" (*uwd*) means, "Do it again." This is a powerful concept to understand and embrace. As you share your testimony of what Christ has done in your life, it's like a prophetic word that releases the power of God to do it again in the lives of the listeners.

There was once a wave of belief in the church that televangelism was going to be the be-all and end-all of reaching the world. Just send your $25 monthly offering and the TV preacher would evangelize the globe for you. However, many scandals later, it is now recognized as only a tool – what it was intended to be all along. God needs each one of us individually to accomplish the task in front of us.

There is one Kingdom and One King. We are His representatives – His ambassadors.

> **2 Corinthians 5:20 Now then, we are ambassadors for Christ, as though God were pleading through us: we implore you on Christ's behalf, be reconciled to God.**

Everywhere we go, we are ambassadors of the Kingdom of God. We are the visible representation of the invisible Kingdom. We have been entrusted with the ministry of reconciliation – to reunite God and man. God is *pleading* through us to lost humanity. The original Greek word for "pleading" (*para-kaleo*) is a compound word and means, "Make a call" from being "close-up and personal." So it is clear that this pleading, this ministry of reconciliation, is primarily done by getting involved in people's lives – personal and up-close.

Share the Good News of the Kingdom wherever you go. Do so conversationally. When the Spirit leads, do so confrontationally. You are an ambassador of the Kingdom – God's official representative.

Other Books by David Chapman

The Fullness of the Spirit
Modern Day Apostles
The Pattern and the Glory
Thus Saith The Lord
The Power of the Anointing
Knowing God's Will
The Power of Praise
The Seven Letters of Jesus
Caught Up
Blood Covenant
The Believer's Deliverance Handbook

www.ingramcontent.com/pod-product-compliance
Lightning Source LLC
Chambersburg PA
CBHW072010040426
42447CB00009B/1569